YORK NOTES

HAMLET

WILLIAM SHAKESPEARE

D0951119

NOTES BY JEFF AND LYNN WOOD

Longman   York Press

For Tom and Sam who were beginning to wonder where their parents were.

Acknowledgements

All students of *Hamlet* are indebted to the armies of scholars and critics who have explored this rich territory. We wish to record our particular indebtedness to three inspiring teachers: Clare Campbell, Stanley Wells and Rex Gibson. Special thanks go to Isabel D. Holowaty, of Cambridge University Library, for her expert assistance when we were preparing the Further Reading section.

Exterior picture of the Globe Theatre reproduced by permission of the Raymond Mander and Joe Mitchenson Theatre Collection
Reconstruction of the Globe Theatre interior reprinted from Hodges; 'The Globe Restored' (1968) by permission of Oxford University Press

The right of Jeff and Lynn Wood to be identified as Authors of this Work has been asserted by them in accordance with the Copyright, Designs and Patents Act 1988

YORK PRESS
322 Old Brompton Road, London SW5 9JH

PEARSON EDUCATION LIMITED
Edinburgh Gate, Harlow,
Essex CM20 2JE, United Kingdom
Associated companies, branches and representatives throughout the world

First published 1998
This new and fully revised edition first published 2003
Third impression 2005

10 9 8 7 6 5 4 3

ISBN 0-582-78428-X

Designed by Michelle Cannatella
Typeset by Land & Unwin (Data Sciences), Bugbrooke, Northamptonshire
Produced by Pearson Education Asia Limited, Hong Kong

CONTENTS

PART FOUR
CRITICAL HISTORY

PART FIVE
BACKGROUND

PART ONE

INTRODUCTION

HOW TO STUDY A PLAY

Studying on your own requires self-discipline and a carefully thought-out work plan in order to be effective.

- Drama is a special kind of writing (the technical term is 'genre') because it needs a performance in the theatre to arrive at a full interpretation of its meaning. Try to imagine that you are a member of the audience when reading the play. Think about how it could be presented on the stage, not just about the words on the page.

- Drama is always about conflict of some sort (which may be below the surface). Identify the conflicts in the play and you will be close to identifying the large ideas or themes which bind all the parts together.

- Make careful notes on themes, character, plot and any sub-plots of the play.

- Why do you like or dislike the characters in the play? How do your feelings towards them develop and change?

- Playwrights find non-realistic ways of allowing an audience to see into the minds and motives of their characters, for example , aside or music. Consider how such dramatic devices are used in the play you are studying.

- Think of the playwright writing the play. Why were these particular arrangements of events, characters and speeches chosen?

- Cite exact sources for all quotations, whether from the text itself or from critical commentaries. Wherever possible find your own examples from the play to back up your opinions.

- Where appropriate, comment in detail on the language of the passage you have quoted.

- Always express your ideas in your own words.

These York Notes offer an introduction to *Hamlet* and cannot substitute for close reading of the text and the study of secondary sources.

QUESTION

How important in *Hamlet* is the idea of play-acting?

READING *HAMLET*

When the Ghost and the Prince meet and everyone ends up in
the mincemeat
                Howard Dietz, 'That's Entertainment', 1953

What mankind have long possessed they have often examined
and compared; and if they persist to value the possession, it is
because frequent comparisons have confirmed opinion in its
favour
                Dr Johnson, *Preface to Shakespeare*, 1765

In all commentating upon Shakespeare there has been a radical
error never yet mentioned. It is the error of attempting to
expound his characters – to account for their actions – to
reconcile his inconsistencies – not as if they were the coinage of
a human brain but if they had been actual existences upon earth.
We talk of Hamlet the man, instead of Hamlet the *dramatis
persona* – of Hamlet that God, in place of Hamlet that
Shakespeare, created. If Hamlet had really lived, and if the
tragedy were an accurate record of his deeds, from this record
(with some trouble) we might, it is true, reconcile his
inconsistencies, and settle to our satisfaction his true character.
But the task becomes the purest absurdity when we deal only
with a phantom. It is not the inconsistencies of the acting man
we have as a subject of discussion…. But the whims and
vacillations – the conflicting energies and indolences of the poet.
It seems to me little less than a miracle that this obvious point
should have been overlooked.
                Edgar Allan Poe, 'Marginalia', *c.*1840

 **CHECK
THE NET**
To find the full
modern text of
Hamlet as a single
page, go to: **http://
the-tech.mit.edu/
Shakespeare/
hamlet/full.html**

Few works of art achieve instant popular acclaim and maintain it
thereafter. Brunelleschi's dome, Mozart's *The Marriage of Figaro*,
Beethoven's Fifth Symphony, Michelangelo's *David*, Shakespeare's
Hamlet have done so. The question is 'How?'

Hamlet is the most popular play ever written. It has been translated
into dozens of languages, is doubtless being performed somewhere

in the world as you read these words, and has been the subject of more excited critical debate than any other work of literature. A catalogue of all the books and articles that have been written on *Hamlet* would fill a CD-ROM. And by the time it was produced, there would be many more commentaries on the play ready for the second release.

How can a work be popular with people who do not think of themselves as 'serious readers' and continue to engage the intellectual energies of the academics? What gives *Hamlet* its purchase upon so many people's interest?

The play was written by Shakespeare around the turn of the seventeenth century. Elizabethan London was a cauldron of unprecedented intellectual and artistic ferment. The atmosphere was politically turbulent and dangerous. But above all the climate was vigorous and experimental. And Shakespeare's art was at the stage when, having brought his poetic technique and his stagecraft to a degree of mastery which aroused in equal measures the envy and admiration of his contemporaries, he was beginning to attempt radical new ways of engaging his audiences.

One reason for *Hamlet*'s enduring popularity is its artistic exuberance. There is no other play which offers such a rich and varied diet of incident, characterisation, subject matter and language. To explore the variety of poetic styles Shakespeare employs in this work would take a sizeable volume. We have magnificent bombastic pastiche when the First Player narrates a riveting episode from the Trojan Wars. There are Ophelia's pretty, plaintive-bawdy songs and the Gravedigger's humorously unsettling one. The Ghost and his widow are given narrative **set pieces** of great power, Gertrude's having generated numerous representations. Claudius has some of the most accomplished rhetoric of any Shakespearean villain, poised on the razor's edge between engaging plausibility and evident hypocrisy. There is Hamlet's moving declaration of love for Horatio and his friend's tender farewell. And as foils to all this eloquence, we have the delicious verbal absurdities of Polonius, Laertes and Osric, Hamlet's biting satire, and the benighted wanderings of

 CHECK THE BOOK

John Dover Wilson describes *Hamlet* as 'a dramatic essay in mystery; that is to say, the more it is examined, the more there is to discover', *What Happens in Hamlet* (1935).

CHECK THE BOOK

'It may seem a paradox, but I cannot help being of the opinion that the plays of Shakespeare are less calculated for performance on stage than those of almost any other dramatist whatsoever. Their distinguished excellence is a reason that they should be so. There is so much in them, which comes not under the province of acting, with which eye, and tone, and gesture, have nothing to do.' Charles Lamb: The *Tragedies of Shakespeare* (1818).

Rosencrantz and Guildenstern. And then, of course, there are the soliloquies of Hamlet and Claudius.

These speeches, above all, give *Hamlet* its distinction and account for some of its absorbing interest. Shakespeare is engaged in the most complex task: to give an audience the illusion that they are listening to two very different people trying to think clearly about fundamental human problems. Although Shakespeare is writing a play, listening to the soliloquies is almost like reading a novel. We are at the edge of what is artistically achievable: presenting genuinely complex, apparently dynamic states of mind intelligibly. Whether theses speeches achieve what they attempt to achieve is genuinely problematic. In exploring them we find ourselves asking fundamental questions about human psychology, epistemology and the nature of language on the one hand, and about the nature of texts and audiences and the challenge posed to the artist who would manipulate such material on the other.

Yet *Hamlet* is never a dry read. It is universally popular because the central character is somebody to whom few people can feel indifferent. For every playgoer or reader who finds Hamlet a prig, a coward or a bully, there are a dozen who earnestly identify with him as a kind of spokesman for their own experience of the bewildering human condition.

It is of little consequence what view we take of Hamlet on first acquaintance; he fascinates us, frustrates any attempt to reduce him to a tidy analysis and demands that we sit through and share his trials again and again. He is fascinating partly because he is so passionately interested in things himself. Like us, he cares about the theatre. He is excited and tested by language and irritated by its misuse. He is by turns full of energy, minting ideas more quickly than others can keep up with, the next dejected and forlorn as he registers his isolation and impotence.

As we grow, Hamlet and his interesting problems grow with us. At one point in the play he says: 'For there is nothing either good or bad but thinking makes it so' (I I.2.239–40). That sentence has many different meanings, several of which operate simultaneously at that moment in the drama. But one thing the words underline is the necessity and the excitement of thinking.

Hamlet urges us to think about so many things.

It is a family drama. Brother and sister, brother and brother, father and son, father and daughter, mother and son, son and stepfather: these are the dynamics which generate so much of the play's electricity. Then we have friendship and friendships betrayed; the nature of duty: to one's country, to those in power, to oneself, to God, to truth. There is the perennially absorbing debate about sexuality and sexual morality, central to any reading of this play. And there is the question of power – of seizing and losing control; the powerlessness of individuals in a world which marginalises them. As society continues to change, the nature of these debates shifts.

And there, perhaps, is the reason why a four-hundred-years-worn text in Elizabethan English continues to excite people from so many different cultures and ideological positions. In this play Shakespeare identifies and dramatises, in colourful, memorable and provocative ways, issues central to everyone's critical self. The question of who we are and why; where we come from, where we have got to and where we will go next. And the degree to which it is possible for any individual to share these investigations with others. The focus shifts continually between gauging the sureness of Shakespeare's craft and responding to the complex, serious and beautiful game he has set in motion between a text and an ever-renewing audience.

We enjoy *Hamlet* as we enjoy watching somebody doing their best to do something all but impossible and, by a whisker, making it. It is not so much a play as a companion for life.

 CHECK THE BOOK

'Though conclusive evidence is hard to come by, it is difficult to read Shakespeare without feeling that he was almost certainly familiar with the writings of Hegel, Marx, Nietzche, Freud, Wittgenstein and Derrida'. Terry Eagleton, *William Shakespeare* (1986).

PART TWO

THE TEXT

NOTE ON THE TEXT

The textual history of *Hamlet* is a long and fascinating one to which a guide of this size can offer only a pointer.

We have none of Shakespeare's manuscripts. A garbled pirated edition of *Hamlet* came out in 1603. It was succeeded by another, much longer version, in 1604, which the printer claimed to be 'according to the true and perfect copy'. In 1623, when a collection of all Shakespeare's plays was printed, the text of *Hamlet* was significantly different from both these earlier texts. The colleagues of Shakespeare who produced this edition claimed the texts to be 'cured, and perfect of their limbs … absolute in their numbers, as he conceived them'.

None of these early editions divides the play into Acts and scenes. Because usually more than one scribe and/or typesetter was involved and Shakespeare's handwriting was notoriously difficult to read, punctuation and spelling are not consistent, even within the same volume.

CHECK THE BOOK

A modernised text of Q1 may be found in *The First Quarto of Hamlet*, ed. Kathleen O. Irace (1998).

Until very recently, editors of Shakespeare usually based their texts upon those published in the First **Folio** of 1623. But where there were earlier versions of the play, two versions in the case of *Hamlet*, what they did was to lift from the earlier versions anything they thought worth including. In the case of *Hamlet*, for example, this meant restoring a major cut in Act IV Scene 4 and recovering some interesting stage directions such as, '*Enter Ofelia playing on a lute, and her hair down, singing*'. They assumed that Shakespeare had written a single version of each play and that the various texts that had come down to us were more or less accurate reproductions of Shakespeare's original.

In the last few years, chiefly as a result of the work of the Oxford editors, it has been agreed generally that Shakespeare revised a number of his plays in the light of what worked on stage and what did not, and to suit changing circumstances in the theatre. *Hamlet* was a play which was immediately popular and was probably given many performances. Like any play in production, Shakespeare probably modified it over a period of time.

Most editors now believe that the 1623 text represents Shakespeare's final acting version of *Hamlet* and that although there are some powerful moments in the earlier **Quartos**, to conflate the three texts, as, for example, Peter Alexander did in his celebrated 1951 edition, is unsound practice. The 1604 Quarto, it is argued, should be regarded a work in its own right: Shakespeare's first version of the play.

It is ironic that Kenneth Branagh's productions of *Hamlet*, one made for BBC Radio and Random House Audiobooks (1992) and the other for Castle Rock films (1997), using the 'complete' text should have come out when there was a strong critical consensus that this conflated text no longer had any authority.

However, since the Alexander text is the one that examination boards continue to prescribe, this guide deals with that spurious but universally popular text. These Notes are based on the Cambridge School Shakespeare edition, 1994, which presents this text and certain variants in the most convenient way for students. Readers should realise that the glosses are our own.

SYNOPSIS

> The incidents are so numerous, that the argument of the play would make a long tale.
>
> Dr Johnson, *Notes on the Plays*, 1765

Apart from Act IV Scene 4 and Act V Scene 1, the whole play takes place inside the castle of Elsinore, seat of the Danish King. The only historical detail is that England is Denmark's tributary, but the court we see and the problems the play explores are thoroughly Elizabethan, not those of the Dark Ages.

CHECK THE BOOK

Students who would like to explore the bibliographical issues are recommended to start by exploring the three versions of *Hamlet* which were published during and immediately after Shakespeare's lifetime. The three texts, the First Quarto, the Second Quarto and the First Folio are most conveniently compared in Paul Bertram and Bernice W. Kliman's excellent edition, *The Three-text Hamlet* (1991), which presents the three versions side by side.

CHECK THE NET

The full texts of Q1, Q2 and the Folio are at: **http://web.uvic. ca/shakespeare**.

**CHECK
THE BOOK**

'The opening scene of *Hamlet* is as well constructed an opening scene as that of any play ever written... What we do not notice... in the theatre, is the great variation of style. Nothing is superfluous and there is no line of poetry which is not justified by its dramatic value...'
T. S. Eliot, *On Poetry and Poets* (1957). Michael Pennington, in his *Hamlet, A User's Guide* (1996) disagrees: 'Wonderfully written as it is, this famous sequence rarely seems to work in the theatre – and not, I think, because of the difficulties of the Ghost.... There must ... be some disheartening problem of belief...'.

Valiant King Hamlet has died; his brother has succeeded him, as King of Denmark and as husband of Queen Gertrude. We see the new King fully in control of the court despite his incestuous marriage. The only discordant note is struck by Prince Hamlet who, alone, is still in mourning for the late King. In a soliloquy, young Hamlet expresses his melancholy and his disgust with the state of affairs. A Ghost closely resembling the late King Hamlet appears on the gun platform of the castle. He commands the Prince to avenge his murder and to cleanse the throne of incest. The Ghost reveals that the murderer was his brother.

Meanwhile, Polonius's daughter, Ophelia, with whom Hamlet is in love, is told by her brother and by her father to end the relationship. She obeys.

The action of Act II takes place some weeks after the events of Act I. Hamlet's behaviour has been odd; the King is disturbed. He sends for Rosencrantz and Guildenstern to spy on him. Learning of a strange visit the Prince has paid his daughter, Polonius tells the King about Ophelia's rejection of Hamlet's advances and suggests that this is the cause of the Prince's 'lunacy' (II.2.49). He reads out a letter Hamlet has sent to Ophelia, and the King and Polonius decide to set up Ophelia so that she and Hamlet can meet where they can eavesdrop on their conversation.

Rosencrantz and Guildenstern admit to Hamlet that they were 'sent for' (II.2.278). Their conversation is interrupted by the arrival of a theatre company Hamlet has long admired. The Prince calls for 'a passionate speech' (II.2.393), giving the actor a cue. Moved by the Player's recitation, Hamlet, alone with the audience, berates himself for his own lack of passion. He has asked the actors to perform a play 'something like the murder of [his] father' (II.2.548). He'll have it performed in front of his uncle so he can observe the King's reactions to test the Ghost's honesty.

In Act III, Polonius's plan is put into action. Ophelia pretends she is reading so Hamlet will not be suspicious. Suddenly Claudius reveals to the audience that he carries a 'heavy burden' (III.1.54) of guilt. Polonius and Claudius hide to listen.

Hamlet delivers the 'To be or not to be' (III.1.56) soliloquy, then
encounters Ophelia. It is unclear at what point he realises she is part
of a conspiracy. Some of his outrage is directed at her, some at the
two men he guesses are listening. Left alone on stage, Ophelia
expresses her sadness at Hamlet's 'ecstasy' (III.1.154) but the King is
convinced his nephew is not mad. He decides to pack off Hamlet to
England. Polonius proposes another snooping session, in the
Queen's room after the play. The King agrees. He wants Hamlet
watched.

The Prince coaches the actors. After a moving declaration of his
love for his friend, Hamlet asks Horatio to observe the King during
the performance. Hamlet sits next to Ophelia so he can watch the
King too. The play is preceded by a mime re-enacting the Ghost's
account of the murder. There is no reaction from the King or the
Queen.

In the first scene of the play, the Player Queen vows vehemently to
be forever faithful to her husband. In the interval, Hamlet asks his
mother's opinion of the play. She replies, 'The lady doth protest too
much, methinks' (III.2.211). The second scene presents the murder
again. Confusingly, Hamlet explains that the murderer is the King's
nephew. Increasingly agitated, Hamlet plays the role of **Chorus**.
When the King rises, displeased, and the performance breaks up in
confusion, it is unclear what has upset the King. Elated, Hamlet asks
Horatio whether the performance would not earn him a share in a
company of players; his punctilious friend responds, 'Half a share'
(III.2.253). However, Hamlet is intoxicated by the experience; in a
soliloquy he imagines taking revenge. Yet it is not the King he
pursues. He goes to his mother's room where he plans to chastise
her.

Hastily the King makes plans to send Hamlet away. Alone,
Claudius struggles to pray; we discover that he is racked with guilt
of his 'foul murder' (III.3, 52). Whilst the King suffers, the Prince
passes him on his way to Gertrude's room. Hamlet has the perfect
opportunity to send the King 'to heaven' (III.3.74). That figure of
speech makes him pause. He cannot kill the King at prayer; he
proceeds to his mother's private apartment.

**CHECK
THE BOOK**

'It is no longer
necessary to stress
that the text of a
play is only its
starting point and
that only in
production is its
potential realized
and capable of
being appreciated
fully... Shakespeare
is only one
collaborator in the
creation and infinite
recreation of his
play upon the
stage...' J.S. Bratton
and Julie Hankey in
*Shakespeare in
Production*, ed.
Robert Hapgood
(1999).

Prompted by Polonius, the Queen attempts to take Hamlet to task for his behaviour to his uncle. Hamlet rounds on her for her offences to his father. Terrified, Gertrude calls for help. Hearing a noise, Hamlet whips out his sword and stabs the man in hiding, believing him to be the King.

CHECK THE BOOK

'The character is consistent. Hamlet is exhibited with good dispositions, and struggling with untoward circumstances. The contest is interesting. As he endeavours to act aright, we approve and esteem him. But his original constitution renders him unequal to the contest: he displays the weaknesses and imperfections to which his peculiar character is liable, he is unfortunate, his misfortunes are in some measure occasioned by his weakness: he thus becomes an object not of blame, but of genuine and tender regret.' William Richardson, *Some of Shakespeare's Remarkable Characters* (1783).

Gertrude accuses him of committing a 'rash and bloody deed' (III. 4.27). Hamlet snaps back that it is not as bad as killing a king and marrying his brother. The Queen's shocked response establishes that she knew nothing of her husband's murder. Her son's denunciation of her sins forces her to acknowledge them. At the emotional climax of their interview, Hamlet is visited a second time by the Ghost who comes to 'whet [his] almost blunted purpose' (III.4.110). Gertrude and Hamlet achieve a new equilibrium. She promises to keep faith with her son.

In Act IV, we see Claudius and Gertrude drawing apart. Neither confides in the other. It serves both their purposes to pretend that the Prince is insane. There is similar play-acting between the Prince and his uncle until the young man is sent off. In a soliloquy, the King reveals he is sending Hamlet to his death.

As Hamlet is about to leave Denmark, he encounters the army of Young Fortinbras. It is off to fight simply for glory. Hamlet's immediate response is disgust. Reflecting a moment later in a soliloquy, however, Hamlet appears to find Young Fortinbras's behaviour glorious, a rebuke of his own lack of action.

Whilst Hamlet is off-stage the focus moves to Ophelia, who has gone mad as a result of her father's death, and then to Laertes. Both the Queen and the King anticipate disaster.

Laertes returns, seeking revenge for his father's death. Calmly, the King agrees to tell him the whole story. Mad Ophelia appears again, to fuel Laertes' passion.

Meanwhile Horatio receives a letter from Hamlet who has escaped from the ship. A second letter reaches Claudius as he is about to reveal to Laertes how he has disposed of Hamlet. United, they plot

Hamlet's death. Gertrude enters and describes Ophelia's death by drowning.

Act V begins in the graveyard, where two sextons discuss Ophelia's suicide. We see Hamlet back from his sea voyage, a different man. He is unaware of the new plot his uncle has laid for him.

Handling the skulls in the graveyard, Hamlet reflects on how death is the great leveller. He meditates on the relative weight of human and divine judgements. Ophelia's funeral procession interrupts him. Laertes' theatrical display of grief so disgusts Hamlet that he mocks Laertes and the two fight by her grave.

Hamlet gives Horatio details of his escape. The experience has convinced him that human destiny is controlled by Providence. Now he feels it would be 'perfect conscience' (V.2.67) to kill the King and damnable to let him live. Hamlet and a foppish courtier generate some of the richest comic moments in the play. The Prince is challenged to a fencing match with Laertes. Although he senses something shady afoot, Hamlet is ready for death, which he feels is all that matters.

The play ends with an exciting and cleverly contrived fencing match conducted in an atmosphere of chicanery. It results in the deaths of all the principal protagonists, followed by brief, powerful tributes to young Hamlet. Horatio is left to tell the Prince's story. Young Fortinbras assumes power in Denmark.

CHECK THE BOOK

Having performed *Hamlet* on the stage, Macready records in his diary: 'End of the play was good. Energy! Energy! Energy!' Macready's Diaries, 1833, in *Responses to Shakespeare*, ed. John Adler (1997).

ACT I

SCENE 1

CONTEXT

'The first audiences who heard and saw this were at the Globe on the Bankside in London in broad daylight at 2 pm, probably on a hot summer's afternoon. They were being asked to imagine that it was the opposite.' For an account of how *Hamlet* would have been presented in 1601, see Andrew Gurr and Mariko Ichikawa *Staging In Shakespeare's Theatres* (2000).

- Barnardo, Horatio and Marcellus take over the watch from Francisco.
- Barnardo and Marcellus tell Horatio about the Ghost that has been seen.
- The Ghost appears; it resembles the late King Hamlet.
- The Ghost reappears and Horatio questions it.
- The men decide to tell Prince Hamlet what they have seen.

Francisco is on watch on the gun platform of Elsinore Castle. It is midnight and Barnardo comes to take over. Francisco is very happy to be relieved: it is bitterly cold and he feels 'sick at heart' (line 9).

As Francisco leaves, he encounters Marcellus and Horatio on their way to join Barnardo. Marcellus asks Barnardo whether 'this thing' (line 21) has appeared again. Horatio is a scholar who has been invited to join the watch. Marcellus has told him about an apparition the sentries have seen twice. Horatio is sceptical. Barnardo begins to tell the story of what they have witnessed.

Suddenly the Ghost appears. It bears a striking resemblance to the late King. Although terrified, Horatio challenges the Ghost, demanding to know why it 'usurps' (line 46) the appearance of the late King. Offended, the Ghost stalks away.

CONTEXT

Mention of 'the most high and palmy state of Rome' (line 13) would have reminded Shakespeare's audience of a dramatic moment in the Globe company's previous tragedy, *Julius Caesar*.

Horatio is shocked; he has lost his scepticism. He interprets the Ghost's appearance as an omen of trouble brewing for Denmark. Acting as narrators, Horatio and Marcellus give the audience the context in which the events of the last few minutes have taken place. Wild young Fortinbras, the nephew of the King of Norway, is threatening to invade, hoping to win back lands surrendered, with full feudal propriety, to King Hamlet.

The Ghost returns. This time Horatio challenges it with three formal questions. It is about to respond when the cock crows. At that sound the Ghost shudders and vanishes.

Horatio and Marcellus comment that evil creatures of the night are driven away by the cockerel, herald of sunrise. As, beautifully, day breaks, the men decide to tell the dead King's son, young Hamlet, what they have seen. They are certain the Ghost will speak to him.

COMMENTARY

Immediately and economically, using fragments of conversation, Shakespeare establishes a mood of anxiety and dread. The verse does not flow. Broken rhythms generate an atmosphere of unease, apprehension and confusion. The play begins with a question and in the next twenty lines come six more. We never learn why Francisco feels 'sick at heart' (line 9): this unexplained phrase anticipates the images of physical and mental illness which colour the whole play. It also prepares us for Prince Hamlet's melancholy in the next scene.

Horatio's credentials as a scholar and a sceptic are established, signalling to the audience that there can be no doubt of the Ghost's existence or of its striking resemblance to the last King of Denmark, the valiant warrior, King Hamlet. The movements of the Ghost, at one moment 'majestical' (line 143) at another 'like a guilty thing' (line 148), establish its ambiguous nature. We cannot tell if it is good or bad or both.

> **CONTEXT**
>
> Claudius's breaking of the fourth commandment, compelling men to work on the Sabbath, would convey to a sixteenth-century Christian audience that this was a modern, pragmatic, Machiavellian king prepared to defy conventional morality.

> **CONTEXT**
>
> The trial of strength between Old King Hamlet and Old King Fortinbras belongs to a world of feudal, chivalric values and behaviour very different from the modern world of pragmatic diplomacy and realpolitik represented by Claudius and Young Fortinbras.

GLOSSARY		
23	fantasy imagination	
29	approve our eyes confirm that our story is true	
44	harrows me tears me apart	
46	usurp'st steals	
48	the majesty of buried Denmark the late King Hamlet	
50	stalks away moves off like someone up to no good	
57–8	the sensible and true avouch / Of mine own eyes having seen it	
65	jump at this dead hour at exactly this time	
66	With martial stalk moving grandly like a great warrior	
68	in the gross and scope of mine opinion as far as I can make it out	
69	bodes some strange eruption signals that something terrible is about to happen	continued

CHECK THE BOOK

The critic Kitteridge notes that Horatio shows a scholar's knowledge of the reasons why, conventionally, a ghost might revisit the earth.

CONTEXT

Marcellus's reference to the celebration of 'our Saviour's birth' (line 159) explicitly identifies Hamlet's Denmark as a Christian country.

74	**foreign mart for implements of war** buying weapons from abroad
83	**pricked on by a most emulate pride** wanting to be thought the greatest
85	**this side of our known world** the whole of Western Europe
90–91	**a moiety competent / Was gagèd by our king** King Hamlet had promised to surrender a similar amount of land if Fortinbras beat him
96	**Of unimprovèd mettle hot and full** uneducated, wild and rash
98-100	**landless resolutes / For food and diet to some enterprise / That hath a stomach in't** men who, having no land themselves, are excited by the idea of fighting for Fortinbras and whatever they may gain as a result
107	**post-haste and romage** frantic activity
118	**the moist star** the moon, whose movements control the tides
121	**precurse of feared events** warning of trouble to come
126	**soft** be quiet, look
128	**If thou hast …** Horatio addresses the Ghost with the three formal questions to which, traditionally, the living dead might respond
140	**partisan** a weapon like a sentry's pike
148	**started** jumped, shuddered
154	**Th'extravagant and erring spirit** the wandering soul of a wicked person who has died
154–5	**hies / To his confine** rushes back to his prison
156	**made probation** proved it to be true
158	**that season …** Christmas Day

SCENE 2

- The new King addresses the court.
- Hamlet is disgusted by the new King (his uncle) and the Queen (his mother).
- The watchmen tell Hamlet about the Ghost.

In the Great Hall of Elsinore Castle, the court is assembled. We learn that in both Denmark and Norway, the dead kings have been succeeded not by their sons but by their brothers. The new King of Denmark has married his brother's widow. Apparently the court has 'freely gone / With this affair along' (lines 15–16) although such a marriage would have been regarded as incestuous by Shakespeare's audience. Confidently and eloquently, the new King deals with four items of business: his accession; the threat from young Fortinbras; Laertes' suit and young Hamlet's dissident behaviour. Claudius deals with Fortinbras's threatened invasion by dispatching ambassadors to the King of Norway, Fortinbras's uncle, ordering him to restrain his nephew. Claudius turns to Laertes, the son of his counsellor Polonius, and grants the young man's request to return to France, as a display of gratitude to Polonius for his services. Finally he confronts Hamlet and is met with a bitter response. Gertrude intervenes only to antagonise Hamlet further. The subject of their differences is Hamlet's continuing to mourn his father whom everyone else, it appears, has forgotten. Claudius vetoes Hamlet's wish to return to Wittenberg. Gertrude turns this into a request. Hamlet obeys his mother. Claudius, having proclaimed Hamlet heir to the throne, leads everyone but Hamlet out of the hall, declaring his pleasure with Hamlet's 'unforced accord' (line 123).

Left alone, Hamlet shares with the audience his wretchedness and his abhorrence of the King and Queen. He tries to come to terms with the recent loss of his father and the indecent haste with which his mother has remarried his uncle, a man utterly unlike his father. He wishes suicide were not a mortal sin. The world has become a tedious, degenerate, foul place, populated only by 'things rank and gross in nature' (line 136). Contrary to the impression given by Claudius and the Queen, we discover that King Hamlet has been dead for only a few weeks.

Horatio, Marcellus and Barnardo arrive to tell Hamlet about the Ghost. After carefully cross-examining them, he agrees to join them on the watch between eleven and twelve.

CONTEXT

Claudius's marriage to Gertrude would have been regarded in Elizabethan times as incestuous and unlawful. Henry VIII divorced Catherine of Aragon believing he had sinned by marrying his brother's widow. It is a union forbidden in Leviticus XVIII.

READ THE BOOK

For a survey of sixteenth-century attitudes to incestuous marriage, see Lisa Jardine ' "No Offence i'the'world": Unlawful Marriage in *Hamlet*' in *Reading Shakespeare Historically* (1996).

CONTEXT

Significantly no one at court but Hamlet is wearing mourning dress; in Shakespeare's time it would be worn for at least a year following the death of a king.

Left alone on stage, Hamlet tells the audience he suspects 'foul play' (line 255).

COMMENTARY

This scene contrasts dramatically with the first. There is light, colour and the whole Danish court assembled in a mood of celebration. The figure of Hamlet stands alone, isolated by his black clothes and evident hostility to the King. (For detailed comment on Claudius's opening speech and his exchanges with Laertes and Hamlet, see the **Extended commentary** on **Text 1**). It is only when the Queen intervenes that Hamlet begins to speak more intelligibly, if still defiantly. Surrounded by people whom he sees acting as if nothing shocking has happened, he is stung by her words: 'Why seems it so particular with thee?' (line 75). He takes this to be an accusation that his mourning is play-acting. Hamlet feels it is his mother who must have been acting the bereaved widow just a week or two previously. Indeed, Gertrude's sentiment 'all that lives must die / Passing through nature to eternity' (lines 72–3) sounds especially insincere because of the trite rhyming couplet. However, Hamlet's first extended speech in the play is significantly addressed to her, signalling to us that she is the person who engages Hamlet's strongest feelings.

CONTEXT

The 'canon 'gainst self-slaughter' (line 132) is the sixth commandment, which forbids all murder, including suicide. Unlike Claudius, Hamlet feels bound by such an injunction.

Shakespeare uses **soliloquy** so Hamlet can share with the audience feelings he could not voice in public. The listless tempo of the words 'How weary, stale, flat and unprofitable' (line 133) conveys his weariness. The speech contrasts dramatically with Claudius's flowing lines. The verse starts and stops, punctuated by expressions of pain and confusion. The disjointed rhythm and dislocated progress of Hamlet's thoughts convey to us his inner turmoil.

The terms in which the Prince thinks of his father are revealing. He was not just an 'excellent' (line 139) king, but superhuman, at the opposite end of the human spectrum from Claudius: 'Hyperion to a satyr' (line 140). The picture Hamlet paints of his father's love for his mother is also on an epic scale: he was so loving to her, 'That he might not beteem the winds of heaven / Visit her face too roughly' (lines 141–2). This conjures up an image of a huge protective figure shielding Gertrude from all dangers. Hamlet's bewilderment and disgust at his mother's hasty remarriage and sexual depravity is revealed in his comparison of her to an experienced post-horse. The disgust is present not only in the imagery but in the sounds of Hamlet's words. Hissing sibilants convey the young man's nausea as, fascinated by the disgusting, he imagines his mother and his uncle in bed together: 'Oh most wicked speed, to post / With such dexterity to incestuous sheets' (lines 156–7). The intensity of Hamlet's disgust here underlines how impossible he finds it to come to terms with the incestuous union of his uncle and his mother and the indecent haste of his mother's re-marriage.

But Hamlet feels bound to suffer in silence: 'But break, my heart, for I must hold my tongue' (line 159). For the audience, Hamlet's words are ironic. They know a Ghost, resembling his father and dressed in steel, is haunting the castle. Even knowing nothing of the conventions of revenge tragedy, the audience would realise that Hamlet will not be permitted simply to suffer.

CONTEXT

Shakespeare's audience would be struck by the parallels with the scandal surrounding Mary Queen of Scots. Mary failed to observe a proper period of mourning for Henry, choosing to remarry a few short months after her husband's death, compounding her disrespect for custom by marrying Bothwell, the man commonly believed to have murdered her husband.

GLOSSARY

	CLAUDIUS Claudius's name appears nowhere in the play, only in the list of characters. We use it in these Notes as an alternative to 'the King' or 'Gertrude's husband' or 'Hamlet's uncle'
3–4	our whole kingdom / To be contracted in one brow of woe the metaphor paints a picture of the whole country with a sad face
5	hath discretion fought with nature good sense has triumphed over natural human feelings
12	dirge a lament for the dead
13	delight and dole happiness and sadness
21	Colleaguèd with this dream of his advantage coupled with this absurd idea that he is now the stronger man
24	with all bands of law in a thoroughly legal way
31	gait advance
64	cousin in Elizabethan times this term covered any near relative
64	my son Hamlet's uncle is now his stepfather too
72–4	common … common wordplay. Gertrude means that it's normal for people to die. Hamlet taunts her with behaving like a 'common' woman, not a Queen continued

79	windy suspiration of forced breath theatrical, phoney sighs
81	dejected haviour of the visage a sad face
92	obsequious sorrow grief appropriate to a funeral
94	impious stubbornness refusing to behave as God would wish
105	the first corse dramatic irony. The first corpse was Abel's. He was murdered by his wicked brother, Cain
115	And we beseech you bend you the **Folio** punctuation inserts a comma after 'beseech you'. Claudius sounds as if he is begging Hamlet to stay in Denmark but the words reveal that the Prince has no choice. Claudius dares not let the son of the man he killed out of his sight
125	jocund health Claudius looks forward to enjoying toasting his stepson with wine
127–8	the heaven shall bruit again / Re-speaking earthly thunder Claudius likes the idea of the Heavens flattering him by echoing all the noise his cannon will make
129	solid/sullied flesh critics have argued for years about whether Hamlet is upset because his flesh is too tough or too dirty
131	the Everlasting God. Hamlet thinks of his eternal before his earthly father
134	all the uses of this world everything on earth
136–7	things rank and gross in nature / Possess it merely there is nothing in it but savage and disgusting creatures
140	Hyperion Hamlet thinks of his father as being like the sun-god, without a blemish
140	a satyr a mythological creature half-man, half-goat, with an insatiable sexual appetite
141	beteem allow
146	frailty, thy name is woman all women are weak
149	Like Niobe, all tears Niobe wept when all her children died, not for her dead husband. It's a revealing remark for Gertrude's son to make
150	that wants discourse of reason lacking language and thus the ability to think
153	Than I to Hercules Hamlet feels he has nothing in common with the mighty mythological hero who carried out apparently impossible tasks
155	gallèd sore

187	all in all perfect in every way
189	I shall not look upon his like again dramatic irony. Soon Hamlet meets the Ghost
192	Season your admiration suspend your disbelief
200	cap-a-pe from head to toe
204	truncheon a general's staff of office
229	beaver visor
247	tenable in your silence kept a secret
255	doubt suspect

SCENE 3

- Laertes warns Ophelia about Hamlet and her own sexuality.
- Polonius gives his departing son advice on how to conduct himself.
- Polonius orders Ophelia to reject Hamlet unless he offers more.

Shakespeare introduces the audience to Polonius's daughter, Ophelia. We learn that 'of late' (line 91) Hamlet has been spending a great deal of time with her and has declared his affection. Laertes is embarking for France and he tells his sister Ophelia to regard Hamlet's love as something unlikely to last and potentially dangerous. Hamlet is young and as he matures, he will change. Besides, as Hamlet is a prince, the King will dictate his choice of a wife. Furthermore, her own sexual feelings are hazardous; young girls are vulnerable to infection. Ophelia promises to heed her brother's advice and says she hopes he will follow it too.

Polonius urges Laertes aboard ship but then takes an extended leave of his son, giving him a list of precepts to follow in France. Laertes bids farewell and Ophelia promises to keep what her brother has said to her a secret.

Polonius asks what the secret is; Ophelia tells him. Polonius instructs her to spend no more time with Hamlet unless he offers her more than he has already. She says she will obey him.

 CHECK THE BOOK
'Certainly this family is much addicted to the giving of earnest advice.' Peter Mercer, *Hamlet and the Acting of Revenge* (1987).

COMMENTARY

The sub-plot of *Hamlet* offers a smaller scale, less intense and less elaborate version of the main plot. After this scene, Polonius and his children, Laertes and Ophelia, are developed almost entirely through their relationships with Claudius, Hamlet and Gertrude. Interestingly, we learn nothing about Ophelia's feelings for Hamlet. She neither says nor does anything to indicate she is unhappy about the instructions given to her by her brother and her father.

Feminist critics cite this scene as evidence of the powerlessness of women in a patriarchy (male dominated world). But Ophelia (whose name means 'serving woman') is dramatically different from many other Shakespearean girls (e.g. Juliet, Desdemona and Cordelia) who resist bullying fathers and even a king.

CHECK THE FILM

In his film of *Hamlet*, Kozinstev shows Ophelia being taught a stiff, formal dance, like a puppet, emphasising her lack of freedom.

To begin with, Laertes sounds as if he is trying to protect his sister from possible disappointment. But as the episode develops, it is fear for the loss of Ophelia's precious 'honour' (line 29), which he compares to 'treasure' (line 31), that appears to concern him. This loss, which would damage the family name, is as likely to come about because of her desire as because of Hamlet's. Laertes' language reveals a fear of sexuality, which reminds us of Hamlet's disgust at his mother's incest in the previous scene.

Polonius's behaviour as a father is now developed. His famous list of precepts to Laertes is full of good sense, eloquently expressed. Only if the director of the play gives us the impression that Laertes has heard it all before does the episode become comic. Laertes leaves the action only to return when things gather towards their tragic climax in Act IV. When we see Polonius alone with his daughter, Shakespeare presents him as authoritarian, insensitive and mercenary. Shakespeare peppers Polonius's speech (lines 106ff) with terms of commercial transactions: 'tenders for true pay ... not stirling ... more dearly ... at a higher rate ...'

GLOSSARY	
1	My necessaries are embarked my belongings are on board
6	a toy in blood a temporary passion

7	**A violet in the youth of primy nature** like a spring flower
11	**nature crescent** as we develop and mature
12	**as this temple waxes** as the body grows
15	**besmirch** stain
22	**circumscribed** controlled by
30	**with too credent ear** believing, trusting too much
31	**your chaste treasure open** surrender your virginity
32	**unmastered importunity** uncontrolled desire
36	**The chariest maid** the shyest, most reserved virgin
36	**prodigal** lavish, taking risks
38	**Virtue itself scapes not calumnious strokes** even good people are slandered
39	**canker** the worm that feeds upon flowers still in bud
47	**as some ungracious pastors do** as some wicked priests do
51	**recks not his own rede** does not follow his own advice
58	**precepts** advice about how to behave
61	**familiar, but by no means vulgar** friendly but not with everyone
62	**their adoption tried** their friendship proved to be reliable
65	**new-hatched, unfledged courage** someone you've only just met
70	**habit** clothes
72	**the apparel oft proclaims the man** you can often judge someone's character from the way they dress
77	**borrowing dulls the edge of husbandry** borrowing money makes people less thrifty
97	**as it behooves my daughter** as my daughter should
103	**tenders** wordplay. Ophelia means 'expressions' (of love), Polonius means 'offers to buy something'
109	**tender me a fool** make me look a fool (whose daughter has been seduced)
110	**importuned** wooed
114	**With almost all the holy vows of heaven** Hamlet has not asked her to marry him
116	**When the blood burns** when you are sexually aroused
128	**Not of that dye … beguile** Polonius says that Hamlet's words are like cheats, pimps, dressed up to look respectable, disguising their immoral intentions

CHECK THE BOOK

'When thrown alone amid harsh and adverse destinies, and amid the trammels and corruptions of society, without energy to resist, or will to act, or strength to endure, the end must needs be desolation. Ophelia – poor Ophelia! O far too soft, too good, too fair, to be cast among the briers of the working-day world, and fall and bleed upon the thorns of life!' Anna Brownell Jameson, *Characteristics of Shakespeare's Women* (1832).

SCENES 4–5

These two scenes are linked.

- Hamlet joins the watch with Horatio and Marcellus.
- The Ghost appears and signals to Hamlet to follow him.
- The Ghost tells Hamlet that he is the spirit of his father, and orders revenge on his murderer, Claudius.
- Hamlet accepts his instruction and vows his friends to secrecy.

CONTEXT
This fascinating 'heavy headed revel' passage was cut from the Folio text, possibly because after the accession of James I, whose wife was Danish, mention of the Danes' reputation for drunkenness might have been regarded as provocative.

CHECK THE BOOK
For a survey of the pervasiveness of images of sickness and disease in *Hamlet*, see Caroline Spurgeon's ground-breaking study, *Shakespeare's Imagery* (1935).

Again, it is midnight and the air 'bites shrewdly' (Scene 4, line 1). On the gun platform Hamlet watches with Horatio and Marcellus. Cannon fire and trumpets 'bray' (Scene 4, line 11) as Claudius observes the drinking custom of Danish kings. Hamlet believes the tradition gives the Danes a bad name abroad and compares it to the case of otherwise deserving men thought disreputable for just one shortcoming.

The Ghost appears, exciting Hamlet into a frenzy of questions. With a 'courteous action' (Scene 4, line 60) the Ghost signals to Hamlet to accompany him to somewhere private. Defying the entreaties of his alarmed companions, Hamlet follows, proclaiming that his 'fate cries out' (Scene 4, line 81).

Horatio and Marcellus go after him. Marcellus believes 'Something is rotten in the state of Denmark' (Scene 4, line 90). Horatio has faith that God will direct things.

Alone with Hamlet, the Ghost tells his story. He says he is the spirit of Hamlet's father, condemned to walk the land by night and suffer the flames of Purgatory by day. Denmark has been deceived. He was not stung by a serpent but poisoned by his brother. When he was asleep in his orchard, Claudius poured poison into his ear. It is not clear from the Ghost's story whether Claudius seduced Gertrude before or after the murder. The Ghost commands Hamlet to avenge the murder and cleanse the throne of the pollution of incest. However, he must leave Gertrude to God's judgement and to the pricks of her conscience. Ironically, the Ghost's parting words are 'Remember me' (Scene 5, line 91).

Hamlet shares his feelings with the audience. He vows to be faithful to the Ghost and forget everything but its 'commandment' (Scene 5, line 102). He is as appalled at his mother's behaviour as he is with Claudius's.

Horatio and Marcellus rejoin Hamlet whose behaviour is excited and whose words are 'wild and whirling' (Scene 5, line 133). Hamlet tells Horatio the Ghost is 'honest' (Scene 5, line 138) and vows his friends to secrecy. When they seem reluctant to swear, the voice of the Ghost sounds from beneath the stage. Horatio and Marcellus promise to say nothing – they will know it is simply an act if Hamlet pretends to be mad.

COMMENTARY

The first part of Scene 4 includes a long speech, later cut by Shakespeare. Hamlet compares the way that the Danish people's reputation abroad is sullied by their infamy for being 'drunkards' (Scene 4, line 19) to faults we often find 'in particular men' (Scene 4, line 23). These lines have given rise to a great deal of critical interest because they appear to provide a formula for Shakespeare's mature tragedies, in which the tragic heroes are men with outstanding qualities compromised by a single tragic weakness. Because the formula fits Macbeth and Coriolanus, the temptation is to try to force Hamlet into the mould. This is to reduce a complex and unusual kind of tragedy, written at a time when Shakespeare's art was developing, to a simplistic and very misleading formula.

> Be thou a spirit of health, or goblin damned.
> Bring with thee airs from heaven or blasts from hell
> Be thy intents wicked or charitable,   (I.4.40–42)

The uncertain identity/moral status of the Ghost and the questionable morality of what it demands of Hamlet is captured in these three antithetical phrases and generates the intellectual energy of Hamlet's dilemma. In reply to his friends' warning not to speak to the Ghost, Hamlet's words: 'I do not set my life at a pin's fee, / And for my soul, what can it do to that …?' (Scene 4, lines 65–6) are profoundly ironic. The Ghost is not life-threatening. The danger it presents is spiritual and psychological, as Horatio anticipates:

CHECK THE BOOK

'Even though the King were trebly a fratricide, in a Christian sense, it would still be a sin to put him to death with one's own hand, without a trial and without justice.' Herman Ulrici, *Shakespeare's Dramatic Art* (1839).

CHECK THE FILM

The words 'some vicious mole of nature' (Scene 4, line 24) have led to an Aristotelian interpretation. Aristotle stated that tragedy was brought about by a weakness of character in the hero. Olivier's 1948 film over-simplifies the play, beginning with the voice-over: 'This is the tragedy of a man who could not make up his mind'.

'What if it tempt you … deprive your sovereignty of reason, / And draw you into madness?' (Scene 4, lines 69ff).

CONTEXT

The Ghost says he was murdered without receiving the last rites which would have absolved him of his sins. Roman Catholics believe that souls can be purified of ordinary human sins through a period of suffering in purgatory and then enter Heaven. Protestants in Shakespeare's audience might have regarded this talk as proof that the Ghost was a devil since they did not believe in purgatory.

We have just seen Ophelia with a father who issued her with instructions that she unquestioningly obeyed. What is striking about Hamlet's behaviour when he is alone with the Ghost is how little *he* says: the Ghost completely dominates the episode. It gives Hamlet a complicated double message and it is upon this equivocation that the dramatic interest of the rest of the play chiefly rests. For a discussion of this, see **The problem of the Ghost**.

Hamlet feels on the brink of madness as a result of what he has been told. The phrase 'In this distracted globe' (line 97) is richly ambiguous, referring to Hamlet's mind, to the world in which he finds himself and also, of course, to the theatre in which the play is being performed. Shakespeare deliberately uses the word 'commandment' (I.5.103) to draw attention to the moral dilemma Hamlet finds himself in. The Ghost's commandment is absolutely at odds with God's. The repetition 'Remember … Remember … remember …' in Hamlet's short **soliloquy** suggests that he fears he may not be able, or wish, to remember what he has been told to do.

CONTEXT

In Shakespeare's Globe, the Ghost would now be calling from 'the cellarage' – the area beneath the stage.

Something that has puzzled many critics is the banter between Hamlet on stage and the Ghost moving about beneath it. Hamlet talks to and about the Ghost in playful, highly disrespectful language: 'boy … truepenny … this fellow in the cellarage … old mole' (Scene 5, lines 150ff). This is a good example of how we can find ourselves asking the wrong questions if we confuse a play with real life. Rather than attempt to make psychological sense of this episode, it is more fruitful to consider Shakespeare's dramatic purposes here. A playwright's job is to suspend the audience's disbelief. But what could be less convincing than someone shouting commands from under the stage pretending to be something supernatural and terrifying? Shakespeare deliberately ridicules the limitations of stagecraft to neutralise the audience's scepticism.

GLOSSARY

Scene 4

8	**takes his rouse** drinks toasts, celebrates
9	**Keeps wassail, and the swaggering up-spring reels** the clumsy words mimic the crude, drunken singing and dancing Hamlet imagines going on
10	**drains his draughts of Rhenish down** heavy alliteration conveys Hamlet's disgust with his uncle's drinking
11	**thus bray out** the trumpets sound gross, like an ass
16	**More honoured in the breach than the observance** it would be more honourable not to observe the custom than to maintain it
18	**traduced and taxed** have a bad reputation
24	**some vicious mole of nature** a moral weakness they were born with
29–30	**some habit that too much o'erleavens / The form of plausive manners** behaviour which is impolite, rude
32	**nature's livery or fortune's star** whether it is a congenital defect or the influence of an unlucky star
36/38	**the dram … scandal** a single shortcoming corrupts and disgraces the whole person
47	**canonised** buried with Christian rites
48	**burst their cerements** flung away the shroud
51	**cast thee up again** vomit
52	**in complete steel** wearing full armour
54	**fools of nature** ordinary human beings
83	**the Nemean lion** a terrifyingly powerful creature subdued by Hercules
	waxes grows

Scene 5

21	**eternal blazon** knowledge of the afterlife, more than mortal knowledge
55	**a radiant angel** the image recalls Hamlet's notion of his father as Hyperion in Act I, Scene 2
56	**Will sate itself** will satisfy itself
57	**prey on garbage** a disgusting picture of Gertrude copulating with Claudius

continued

CHECK THE BOOK

Peter Stallybrass (in Howard and Shershow, 2001) argues that: 'In figuring his father as mole [Scene 5, line 161ff.], Hamlet enacts a radical metamorphosis: from human to animal; from omnipotent monarch to blind burrower; from ideological figurehead to a worker in the ground. It is a literal humbling, a bringing of the ideological super-structure down to earth "humus", the etymological root for "humble" is the Latin for "earth".'

CONTEXT

Hamlet says *'Hic et ubique'* (Latin, meaning 'here and everywhere', I.5.156). This is ironic, given the ambiguous status of the Ghost, since it is a term commonly applied by Christians to God, thought to be everywhere at all times.

CHECK THE BOOK

Lines 189–90, Goethe says, hold 'the key to Hamlet's whole procedure … The effect of a great action laid upon a soul unfit for the performance of it' (*Wilhelm Meister's Apprenticeship*, 1796). Heiner Muller calls Hamlet 'an intellectual who is no longer certain how to behave and what to do: the old things don't work any more but the new ways aren't to his taste' (quoted in Robert Hapgood (ed.) *Shakespeare in Production* (1999).

CONTEXT

Some critics have suggested that Polonius's pompous and overbearing behaviour in this scene might have made Shakespeare's audience think of Queen Elizabeth's chief minister, Lord Burghley.

62	**cursèd hebenon in a vial** deadly poison in a small bottle
66	**swift as quicksilver it courses through** the movement of the words imitates the rapid progress of the poison through the system
68	**doth posset / And curd, like eager droppings** the movement is arrested as we imagine the blood curdling
77	**Unhouseled, disappointed, unaneled** there was no opportunity to prepare the soul for death, no priest to administer the last rites
87	**waxes** grows

ACT II

SCENE 1

This scene takes place some weeks after the events of Act I.
- Polonius sends Reynaldo to spy on his son.
- Ophelia reports Hamlet's strange appearance and behaviour to Polonius.

Polonius sends a spy, Reynaldo, to observe how his son, Laertes, is behaving in Paris.

As Reynaldo leaves, Ophelia rushes in to tell Polonius about a strange visit Hamlet has paid her. His clothes filthy and dishevelled, his knees knocking and his face pale with horror, he entered Ophelia's room and examined her face minutely. He said nothing but with a 'piteous and profound' sigh (line 92), left the room, his eyes fixed on Ophelia. Polonius interprets this as the behaviour of a rejected lover and Ophelia confirms that she has not only refused to see Hamlet but has gone further and rejected his letters. Believing he has discovered what is upsetting Hamlet, Polonius hurries to tell the King.

COMMENTARY

The episode with Reynaldo is there partly to signal to the audience that some weeks have passed since the end of Act I. Laertes has been in Paris long enough to need more money. The name 'Reynaldo', suggesting fox-like, draws attention to the sly and underhand tricks Polonius tells his man to use in Paris. The words 'let him ply his music' (line 71) imply that Polonius hopes Reynaldo will catch Laertes doing something reprehensible. His tactics – 'by indirections [to] find directions out' (line 64) – anticipate those that the King and his spies, Rosencrantz and Guildenstern, will use when they attempt to discover what Hamlet has on his mind.

However, in this scene, Shakespeare lightens the tone by developing a side of Polonius which makes him not simply unpleasant but enjoyably ludicrous too. Full of his own importance and intoxicated by words, he has a tendency to lose the thread of his argument: 'what was I about to say? / By the mass I was about to say something. Where did I leave?' (lines 49–50). Each director of *Hamlet* has to decide how much of a buffoon, how much of a tyrant to make Claudius's chief courtier appear.

The way Polonius deals with his daughter, showing no interest in what she is feeling, reminds us of the Ghost's one-sided conversation with Hamlet in the previous scene.

Ophelia describes Hamlet's look as 'so piteous in purport / As if he had been loosèd out of hell / To speak of horrors' (lines 80–3). It would be easy to assume that he has come straight from the terrible encounter with the Ghost. He has not and it is important that the audience realises that some weeks have passed since that encounter. From the way she has treated him, Hamlet knows Ophelia will immediately tell her father what has happened and that he will relay it all to the King. Here again, feminist critics comment that Ophelia seems to have no scope for following her own wishes. Others, contrasting her with Juliet, accuse her of a complete lack of spirit.

> **CONTEXT**
>
> Polonius alludes to two Elizabethan games: 'tennis' (line 58), by which he means real tennis, considered a disreputable pastime; and bowls, from which his elaborate metaphor comes: 'with windlasses and with assays of bias, / By indirections find directions out' (lines 63–4) – a skilful player's bowl follows a curved trajectory to reach the target.

CHECK THE FILM

See the way Kozintzev re-presents Ophelia's account of Hamlet's distracted behaviour.

GLOSSARY

7	**Danskers** Danish people
20	**forgeries** lies
24	**gaming** gambling
26	**drabbing** using prostitutes
30	**incontinency** sexual excess (using too many prostitutes)
31	**breathe** suggest
34	**A savageness in unreclaimèd blood, / Of general assault** the passionate wildness most young men suffer from
38	**fetch of warrant** a legitimate trick
39	**laying these slight sullies on my son** accusing my son of these trivial slips
43	**the prenominate crimes** these crimes we have been talking about
60	**Videlicet** that is to say
75	**closet** private apartment
76	**unbraced** undone, loose
100	**the very ecstasy of love** exactly how a distraught lover behaves
110	**quoted him** watched him
111	**beshrew my jealousy** curse my suspicious nature

SCENE 2

- Rosencrantz and Guildenstern arrive to spy on Hamlet.
- The King allows Fortinbras to march his forces across Denmark.
- Following Polonius's advice, the King plans a meeting between Hamlet and Ophelia on which he and Polonius will eavesdrop.
- Hamlet taunts Polonius.
- Hamlet forces Rosencrantz and Guildenstern to confess they were sent for.
- The First Player delivers the Hecuba speech.
- In his second soliloquy, Hamlet berates himself and anticipates *The Mousetrap*.

Disturbed by Hamlet's 'transformation' (line 5), Claudius has summoned two former school friends of Hamlet's to spy on him. Like Ophelia, two of Hamlet's oldest friends, Rosencrantz and Guildenstern, readily conspire with the King against him, this time for personal profit.

The ambassadors return. The King of Norway has halted his nephew's expedition against Denmark. With Claudius's permission, Young Fortinbras will now march across Denmark to do battle in Poland.

Polonius announces to the King and Queen that he has discovered the cause of Hamlet's 'lunacy' (line 49). In an aside to Claudius, Gertrude reveals some understanding of her son's 'distemper' (line 55) and acknowledges that their marriage was 'o'erhasty' (line 57). Polonius reads part of a letter Hamlet sent to Ophelia. It is a puzzling mixture of bitter taunt and clumsy sincerity and anticipates the charges of using cosmetics he will make against her in the 'nunnery' episode. Polonius tells the King and Queen how he has put an end to the young couple's relationship. Claudius, eager to test whether this is the cause of Hamlet's odd behaviour, agrees to Polonius's plan that they should eavesdrop on a contrived meeting between Ophelia and Hamlet.

We see Hamlet for the first time since his 'transformation' (line 5). He and Polonius have a conversation. As Polonius takes his leave, Hamlet again expresses his desire to die.

Rosencrantz and Guildenstern greet Hamlet. There is some witty banter in which we catch a glimpse of Hamlet's former intellectual energy. Then, sensing his friends' unease, he makes them confess that they were sent for by the King. Hamlet confides to them that he feels the delight has gone out of life and that Denmark is like a 'prison' (line 234). He tells them he's giving nothing away to his 'uncle-father and aunt-mother' (line 345) and warns them he is 'but mad north-north-west' (line 348): that he is mad only occasionally. Rosencrantz and Guildenstern tell the Prince about the distinguished company of actors which will arrive shortly. They are on the road, forced to tour because of changing fashions. Hamlet says that this is to be expected with his uncle on the throne.

 CHECK THE BOOK
Hamlet may simply be talking nonsense but **'fishmonger'** (line 172) was Elizabethan slang for 'brothel keeper'. Polonius is abusing his daughter to serve his own ends. For a study of the prevalence of the theme of prostitution in *Hamlet*, see *'Hamlet's Whores'* by Kay Stanton in *New Essays on Hamlet*, ed. Mark Thornton Burnett and John Manning (1994).

CONTEXT

Lines 306ff contain
one of the most
striking topical
allusions in the
whole of
Shakespeare's
output.
Shakespeare's
Globe company
was engaged in
intense rivalry
with other
theatres, including
one employing
boy actors, 'an
**eyrie of children,
little eyases'** (line
315). The boys
were so popular in
London that some
adult companies
had to go on tour
to find audiences.

The actors arrive and, at the Prince's request, the Principal Player
recites a powerful poem. It is Hamlet's favourite episode from the
Trojan War. Significantly, the passage which Hamlet finds most
appealing focuses not on the slaughter of the King but on the
moving grief of his loyal Queen, Hecuba. Hamlet asks the actors to
stage *The Murder of Gonzago* the following night, for which he will
supply an extra speech.

Hamlet's enthusiasm for the 'Hecuba' speech leads him into
examining his present state of mind in the second major soliloquy
Impressed by the simulated passion of the actor, Hamlet feels
inadequate and ashamed of his delay in avenging his father's death.
In the second half of the speech, Hamlet expresses, for the first time,
doubts about the Ghost's honesty and intentions: 'The spirit that I
have seen / May be a devil' sent 'to damn me' (lines 551ff). He
resolves to test the truth of the Ghost's story by having the actors
perform a play which closely re-presents the Ghost's account of his
murder. Guilty people watching plays have been shocked into
confessing their crimes. Hamlet hopes the play will give him some
proof that the Ghost was telling the truth and that it will provoke
Claudius into revealing his guilt. 'The play's the thing / Wherein I'll
catch the conscience of the king' (lines 557–8).

COMMENTARY

The mock-incredulous tone of Claudius's words: 'What it should be, /
More than his father's death, that thus hath put him / So much from
th'understanding of himself, / I cannot dream of' (lines 7ff), suggests
that the King fears Hamlet may suspect foul play. So, when he speaks
of finding a 'remedy' (line 18) for Hamlet's affliction, Claudius may be
already wondering if he will have to get rid of this potential avenger.

The return of the ambassadors serves two distinct purposes. It
demonstrates Claudius's political wisdom. He has dealt with the
military threat from Norway as effectively as his brother would have
done, apparently at far less risk to the country. But the news that
Fortinbras will march across Denmark on his way to fight the Poles
anticipates his army's triumphal return at the very end of the play. As a
direct result of Claudius's crimes, Young Fortinbras will gain control
of Denmark as his father failed to do. For Denmark, Claudius's reign,

beginning with regicide, will be an even greater disaster than Macbeth's was for Scotland. The kingdom will fall into foreign hands.

One of the difficulties facing each director of the play is to decide exactly when Hamlet comes on stage in this scene and how much, if any, of the plotting between Claudius and Polonius he overhears. John Dover Wilson, in *What Happens in Hamlet*, suggests that Hamlet overhears this conversation.

Hamlet's words to Polonius are cryptic. They recall his exchanges with Claudius in Act I Scene 2. What sounds like nonsense has a thread of bitter satire running through it. His remarks to Polonius are not madness, but forthright contempt, privileged rudeness in a court where no one speaks the truth.

> … for there is nothing either good
> or bad but thinking makes it so   (II.2.239–40)

Hamlet's famous line has many possible meanings. He probably does not believe, as he seems to, that all truth is relative; rather, that humans have a duty to use their God-given reason to think and thus work out the difference between good and bad. The subtlety is lost on his companions.

Hamlet's enthusiastic response to the news of the actors' imminent arrival: 'He that plays the king shall be welcome' (line 298) is interesting. The rest of that sentence can sound like an afterthought, intended to cover his tracks. Perhaps some vague idea of putting on *The Mousetrap* occurs spontaneously to him. Like the arrival of Horatio, and even of Rosencrantz and Guildenstern, the boisterous entry of the Prince's favourite actors breathes new life into *Hamlet*, emphasising how like a prison Elsinore is. All vitality comes from outside.

CONTEXT

Hamlet's celebration of humanity's capacity for achieving wonderful things in his 'What a piece of work is a man!' speech (lines 286–92) is a theme of much Renaissance literature. Here, the note of exultation quickly exhausts itself to give way to the scathing/dejected tone of 'Man delights not me'.

 CHECK THE FILM

Notice the way in which Kozinstev's magnificent film of *Hamlet* continually reinforces the idea of Elsinore as a prison, with its imagery of massive stone walls, bars, the heavy portcullis and Ophelia's severely regulated behaviour.

GLOSSARY	
13	vouchsafe your rest agree to stay
21	to whom he more adheres of whom he is fonder
22	gentry Gertrude flatters Rosencrantz and Guildenstern by crediting them with the manners of gentlemen continued

30	in the full bent absolutely, completely
59	brother Norway fellow king
62	levies soldiers
63	the Polack Poland
67	falsely borne in hand tricked, deceived
109	celestial … soul's idol hyperbole is not typical of Hamlet
112	*et cetera* things indecent to repeat
121–2	whilst this machine is to him as long as I live
124	solicitings wooing
134	played the desk, or table-book acted as go-between
137	round firmly
139	out of thy star from a higher social class
154	Take this from this an implied stage direction. Polonius points to his head then to his torso
161	arras a large, heavy tapestry
163	I'll loose my daughter to him a particularly gross term for Polonius to employ, 'loose' being commonly used of setting a cow to a bull for mating
168	board a pun. Polonius is thinking about someone boarding a ship. But the word sounds like 'bawd': a pimp
179	if the sun breeds maggots … carrion even the sun, which we think of as God-like and pure, breeds maggots in corrupt flesh
182	Conception getting pregnant
184	harping on thinking about
193–6	old men … hams a grotesque but probably accurate picture of Polonius
203	pregnant perceptive, clever, witty
229	doomsday the Day of Judgement when everyone must tell the truth
244	have bad dreams … I am most dreadfully attended Hamlet is thinking of the visit of the Ghost
282–3	sterile promontory a place where nothing will grow
286–90	What a piece of work is a man … quintessence of dust Hamlet paints a wonderful picture of humanity's infinite potential only to conclude that now he feels that man is insignificant and worthless
296	coted overtook
301–2	tickle o'th'sere made to laugh easily (a metaphor taken from pistols with very light triggers)

CONTEXT

The words 'lenten entertainment' (line 305) mean 'a miserable reception': Elizabethan theatres were closed during Lent, the period between Ash Wednesday and Easter marked in Christian countries as a time of abstinence, in commemoration of Christ's fast in the wilderness.

302	the lady shall say her mind freely on stage a woman can be given more freedom to express her views than she may have in everyday life
309	the late innovation the latest fashion (i.e. for boy actors)
315	eyeases (spiteful) little hawks
321	escoted looked after
321	no longer than they can sing until their voices break
324	exclaim against their own succession by fuelling the fashion, the boys will find themselves out of work when they grow up
327	tar them to controversy encourage them to fight (as dogs were)
333	Hercules and his load the emblem of Shakespeare's own theatre, the Globe
335	make mouths pull faces
341	appurtenance of welcome the proper way to welcome friends
342	garb fashion, way
348	a hawk from a handsaw two things utterly unlike one another, 'as different as chalk and cheese'
355	You say right sir, a Monday … Hamlet is making small talk
360	Buzz, buzz Hamlet makes a rude noise: the news is stale
363	for tragedy … historical-pastoral Shakespeare mocks pedants who, like Polonius, try to force plays into categories
368	Jephtha a rash character in the Old Testament who sacrificed his daughter
380	As by lot … a snatch of a popular ballad about Jephtha
384	abridgement interruption
386	valanced fringed (he's grown a beard)
387	to beard me to challenge me (by tugging my beard)
389	a chopine a high-heeled shoe
390	uncurrent gold a cracked coin had no value
397	caviary to the general too good to be popular, 'like pearls before swine'
400	set down with as much modesty as cunning the playwright didn't try to show off how clever he was
401	sallets tasty bits, sexual innuendoes
408	Hyrcanian beast a ferocious tiger
414	heraldry more dismal he has smeared his face with blood
	continued

CONTEXT

Hamlet talks about his step-father's valuable 'picture in little' (line 348). Exquisite miniature portraits were highly prized in Elizabethan England. Nicholas Hilliard was the master of the craft.

CONTEXT

Seneca and Plautus (line 366) were, respectively, the Roman masters of tragedy and comedy.

CONTEXT

When Hamlet greets 'my young lady' (line 388) we are reminded that he is speaking to a boy who was playing the female roles.

CONTEXT

Traditionally, at the end of performances at the Globe, even of tragedies, four actors dressed as men and women would perform a jig (see line 458) – usually a bawdy song and dance routine.

415	Now is he total gules covered in blood (gules is the red used in heraldry)
417	Baked and impasted the dried blood is like the crust of a pie
420	o'er-sizèd with coagulate gore the ugly sound of the words increases the horror of what is being described, a man made bulkier by the gore sticking to him
421	carbuncles fiery red jewels
429	Repugnant to command too heavy to lift
431	the whiff and wind of his fell sword the words evoke the noise the terrifying sword makes as it cuts through the air
432–4	senseless Ilium … with a hideous crash the buildings of the city of Troy fall to the ground in sympathy with Priam, even though you would not expect a city to feel things
442	the rack stand still the clouds calm before the storm
447	Cyclops giant blacksmiths who made armour for the gods
458	a jig a comic interlude or dance
461	mobled muffled. Polonius praises the use of this obscure word!
464	bisson rheum her eyes blinded by her tears
466	o'er-teemèd loins a body exhausted from having borne so many children
471	make malicious sport / In mincing Shakespeare imitates the old-fashioned alliterative effect used to generate horror
475	made milch the burning eyes of heaven made the stars in the heavens weep in sympathy
485	God's bodkin a mild expletive, 'by God's sweet body'
504	a dream of passion where he is pretending to be suffering terribly
505	conceit thoughts, imagination
506	visage wanned face went deathly pale
508	his whole function all his movements, his energy
515	cleave the general ear burst everyone's eardrums
519	muddy-mettled feeble, lacking spirit
520	unpregnant of my cause forgetting what I'm supposed to be doing
522	property and most dear life his own precious body
524	pate skull
529	pigeon-livered, and lack gall a pigeon's liver would produce no gall to make someone furious enough to take revenge

CONTEXT

The grandiloquent speech that Hamlet recites is written in a quaint, old-fashioned blank verse style parodying that of Shakespeare's popular predecessor, Christopher Marlowe. Hamlet chooses a moment from a revenge play. Like Hamlet, Pyrrhus was a son out to avenge the slaughter of his father.

531	kites flesh-eating birds
535	most brave a splendid bit of acting!
539	drab whore
540	scullion the lowest kind of kitchen servants, known for their foul language
545	proclaimed their malefactions blurted out their evil deeds
550	tent him to the quick a surgical metaphor 'probe him to the bottom of his wound' (a painful procedure)
550	blench flinch with pain
557	More relative than this more convincing than the Ghost's story alone

ACT III

SCENE 1

This scene takes place the next day.

- Hamlet's 'crafty madness' is discussed. Claudius reveals his guilt.
- Hamlet delivers his third soliloquy: 'To be or not to be ...'.
- Claudius and Polonius eavesdrop on Ophelia and Hamlet's conversation which breaks up in bitterness.
- Ophelia expresses her despair.
- Claudius resolves to deal with Hamlet by sending him to England.

Claudius debriefs Rosencrantz and Guildenstern. He now talks of Hamlet's 'turbulent and dangerous lunacy' (line 4). Guildenstern accuses Hamlet of 'crafty madness' (line 8). Claudius looks forward to watching the play. Ophelia is set up so Hamlet may encounter her. Gertrude hopes Ophelia's beauty is the cause of her son's 'wildness' (line 40) and that her virtue will restore him. Unwittingly Polonius's words give Claudius's conscience a lash; he reveals to the audience he carries a heavy burden of guilt.

Hamlet delivers the 'To be or not to be' (line 56) **soliloquy**

CHECK THE FILM

The staging of this scene poses interesting problems for every director. At what point does Hamlet realise that a trap has been laid, that Ophelia is lying and that the King and Polonius are listening? Watch as many different versions of the scene as you can, noting exactly how the director conveys to us the moment at which Hamlet's suspicions are aroused and how he reacts.

Hamlet and Ophelia meet for the first time in the play. Ophelia's manner is stiff; Hamlet quickly becomes suspicious and then contemptuous. He asks her if she is 'honest' (line 103) and comments on how easily beauty makes good people bad. He tells Ophelia to go and live in a 'nunnery' (line 119). When she tells him a direct lie, Hamlet explodes with fury, directed partly at her, partly as those he guesses are listening.

Alone with the audience, Ophelia talks of her despair at Hamlet's 'ecstasy' (line 154).

Claudius is alarmed by what he has heard. Convinced that his nephew is a threat, he acts with 'quick determination' (line 162) and decides to ship him off to England. Polonius proposes spying on Hamlet again, this time in his mother's room. Claudius agrees, pretending again that he thinks Hamlet is mad and therefore needs watching.

COMMENTARY

Claudius's concern that Rosencrantz and Guildenstern should come up with something beyond Polonius's diagnosis reveals his own state of mind before *The Mousetrap* and prepares us for his agonised soliloquy.

His unexpected, powerful and shocking aside shows him to be a much more psychologically developed and interesting character than the bland smiler he appeared in Act I Scene 2. The imagery he uses makes the necessary connection between the part Ophelia is playing and his own deceptions.

Hamlet's soliloquy

The dramatic purpose of this all too familiar episode is to establish Hamlet as characteristically detached, reflective, analytic, thinking and moral – as somebody temperamentally unlike the active, simple-minded figures of Old Hamlet, Fortinbras and his son, and the rash Laertes. Just a few hours before the play designed 'to catch the conscience of the king' (II.2.558) is to be performed, we see its impresario absorbed in abstract reflection.

CHECK THE BOOK

'No one but Shakespeare could have interrupted an exciting dramatic intrigue with a passage like this.' (Dover Wilson, *What Happens in Hamlet*, 1935) 'Unlike the other soliloquies, this one shows no sign of belonging to the particular scene in which it appears.' (L. L. Schücking, *The Meaning of Hamlet*, 1939) Many critics have observed that there is nothing in this famous soliloquy which has any direct bearing on the action of the play.

The metaphor at the start, 'take arms against a sea of troubles, / And by opposing end them' (lines 59–60) is deliberately confused. It captures Hamlet's feelings of being unequal to the task that has been assigned to him. He feels that trying to set the world to rights would be like committing suicide.

The rest of Hamlet's speech is fluent; it might be something he is reading. It says nothing about his immediate situation, never uses the words 'I' or 'me', but reflects dispassionately, in general terms on how tempting it is to try and escape the wretched human condition. There is no mention of the Ghost, of the play about to be performed, of Hamlet's father's murder or his mother's behaviour. Everything is generalised into a bleak but surprisingly calm, philosophical consideration of the popular Renaissance theme of whether our troublesome life is worth living. Perhaps, as Q1 suggests and Ophelia pretends to be doing, Hamlet is 'poring upon a booke' (line 109). The ideas it explores are expressed as general truths: 'Thus conscience does make cowards of us all' (line 83).

In Hamlet's most famous **soliloquy**, there is no word about his father, his mother, his uncle or any plans for revenge. And when we hear death described as: 'The undiscovered country from whose bourn / No traveller returns' (lines 79–80), it seems as if Hamlet has forgotten that not long ago a figure, strikingly like his father, was telling him about the horrors of purgatory. If the audience can still hear the Ghost's words 'Remember me' (I.5.91), Hamlet it seems cannot. This soliloquy is very unlike the others Shakespeare gives Hamlet. There is a dejected uniformity of tone and tempo, none of the passionate agitation associated with someone wrestling with complex and confused feelings. As a result, it serves as a powerful dramatic contrast to the passionate exchanges which follow.

The 'nunnery' episode

There are striking structural similarities between Hamlet's conversation with Ophelia here and the one he has with Gertrude in Act III Scene 4. The emotional structure of the two episodes differs, however, because of the presence throughout this one of Claudius and Polonius. In Act III Scene 4 the eavesdropper is removed at the

CHECK THE BOOK

Alex Newell describes Hamlet's soliloquy as 'entirely motivated by reason, untouched by passion. In its academic method and style, the speech carries the stamp of Hamlet's identity as a student, formally posing a "question" or topic for debate' (*The Soliloquies of Hamlet*, 1991).

CONTEXT

Earlier Hamlet called Polonius a 'fishmonger' (II.2.172). Ophelia's unfortunate use of the word 'commerce' (line 109) triggers the prostitution association again. When Hamlet advises Ophelia to go to a 'nunnery' (lines 119ff), he may be suggesting she enter a convent to escape the corrupt world of Elsinore or, believing she has sold herself already, suggesting she work in a brothel, 'nunnery' being Elizabethan slang for such a place.

beginning of the meeting. In this episode it is the listeners who effectively send Hamlet away at the end.

It is significant that although Gertrude is on stage during the planning of this unsavoury spying episode, she takes no part in it. This helps the audience to focus upon Claudius as Hamlet's enemy and prepares us for Gertrude's gradual change of allegiances in the second half of the play. Gertrude moves from being Claudius's accomplice to being Hamlet's ally; Ophelia from appearing to be Hamlet's friend to revealing herself as nothing but Claudius's tool.

Hamlet's immediate response to coming so unexpectedly upon the Ophelia he has been unable to talk to for weeks is gentle. The very sounds of his words 'Soft … fair Ophelia … Nymph … orisons …' (lines 88–9) suggest a tender, not an aggressive instinctive reaction to so unexpectedly discovering her.

As he catches sight of Ophelia, Hamlet describes her as 'fair' (line 89), the word he will use to describe her at her funeral. It is a word of particular weight in Shakespeare. In the Sonnets, 'Fair, kind and true' describe the qualities which we most admire in those we love: beauty, honesty, gentleness, truthfulness and loyalty. Certainly Ophelia looks 'fair'. Hamlet has hitherto regarded her as lovely in appearance *and* character.

But no sooner has Ophelia begun to speak, in a manner that is formal, forced and self-conscious because she knows that Claudius and Polonius are listening to every word, than Hamlet's doubts about her honesty are aroused. Feeling tricked, he becomes contemptuous and threatening. He asks Ophelia directly if she is what she appears to be: 'Are you honest? … Are you fair?' (lines 103 and 105).

Hamlet is puzzled, frustrated and wounded that having at last allowed him access, her impersonal language should block any proper communication between them. He does not set out to attack her; she begins by treating him as if he were somebody else. She is acting, posing as his wronged sweetheart in the process of betraying him to his enemy.

If we believe Hamlet when he says in Act V that he 'loved Ophelia' (V.1.236) then we can understand why he is so shocked by her betrayal of him. In his disappointment, Hamlet's disgust with her becomes, as with his mother, focused upon sexual depravity. He sees Ophelia as a whore, as frailty personified rather than as a particular woman: 'I have heard of your paintings ... You jig, you amble ... and make your wantonness your ignorance' (lines 137ff).

It is not clear from the text at what point Hamlet realises he is being tricked and listened to. Certainly by the time Ophelia lies to him by telling him that her father is 'at home' (line 127), Hamlet knows he is being set up.

Each director of the play must decide which of Hamlet's words should be directed at Ophelia and which at those listening from behind the arras. However, there can be no doubt that what he says at the end of this episode, 'Those that are married already, all but one shall live' (lines 141–2), is a direct provocation of the King. It is the closest Hamlet gets to playing a **revenge hero**

CHECK THE BOOK

For a critical analysis of distinctive patterns in the language of *Hamlet,* see Frank Kermode's book *Shakespeare's Language* (2000).

CHECK THE FILM

Does Ophelia hear Hamlet's famous soliloquy? In one production, Derek Jacobi clasps Ophelia's knees as he delivers the speech.

GLOSSARY	
1	by no drift of circumstance indirectly
2	puts on Claudius's metaphor suggests he thinks Hamlet is acting
13	Niggard of question not very talkative
17	o'er-raught passed
29	closely secretly
32	Lawful espials Claudius tries to make his underhand behaviour seem responsible
45–6	colour / Your loneliness explain why you are here all alone. The word 'colour' suggests someone using cosmetics
47	with devotion's visage looking as if we are doing something holy
48	sugar o'er / The devil himself disguise the foulest things
50	How smart a lash that speech doth give my conscience Claudius compares himself to a harlot being whipped through the streets for her sins
51	beautied artificially beautified, painted with cosmetics
53	most painted word hypocrisy continued

CONTEXT

When Hamlet says
'there's the rub'
(line 65) he means
'something that
gets in the way';
the metaphor
comes from the
game of bowls.

57	suffer put up with
63	a consumation devoutly to be wish'd a very appealing end to everything
67	shuffled off this mortal coil the image compares a person shaking off all of life's worries with a snake shedding its skin
71	contumely sneering, contempt
73	dispriz'd rejected, unvalued
74	the spurns / That patient merit of the unworthy takes the criticisms good people have to put up with from people far less decent
76	a bare bodkin a naked dagger
76	fardels loads, burdens
79	bourn boundary
84	hue of resolution the colour in the cheeks of a determined person
86	pitch and moment magnitude and importance
88	soft you now be quiet
89	orisons prayers: Ophelia is pretending to read from the Prayer Book
101	Rich gifts … unkind Ophelia is accusing Hamlet of being unfaithful
103	honest (i) telling the truth (ii) sexually pure
107–8	admit no discourse have nothing to do with
109	commerce Ophelia means 'dealings' but Hamlet hears it as 'trade'
117	inoculate our old stock graft onto the sins we inherit
117	relish of it display our fallen nature, behave badly
119	indifferent fairly
134	what monsters you make of them a cuckold is a man whose wife has slept with another man. He was pictured as having animal horns growing from his temples
137	paintings using cosmetics: putting on a false face, lying
138–9	jig … amble … lisp … nickname God's creatures affected behaviour, all designed to be seductive
139–40	make your wantonness your ignorance pretend that you do not know what you are up to

SCENE 2

This scene happens some hours later.

- Hamlet makes preparations for the play, with which he will test the truth of the Ghost's story.
- The play is performed; Hamlet and Horatio observe the King's reaction to it.
- Hamlet is summoned to the Queen's room.

Hamlet is coaching the actor who will deliver his lines. He reveals a passionate interest in and expert knowledge of the theatre.

Alone with Horatio, Hamlet expresses his admiration for his one trustworthy friend. He asks Horatio to observe Claudius's looks during the scene in which the murderer pours poison into the king's ear so that afterwards they can compare notes and judge the truth of the Ghost's story.

Hamlet sits by Ophelia to watch the play and observe his uncle. He continues to slash verbally at Claudius, Polonius and Ophelia. Ophelia confirms that Hamlet's father has been dead less than six months.

The performance begins with a mime closely modelled on the Ghost's account of his murder. Ophelia does not understand it; there is no reaction from anyone else.

The play proper begins. The Player King and Player Queen have been married for thirty years. The Player King's health is failing and he predicts that when he is dead, his wife will remarry. She asserts that such a marriage would be 'treason' (line 159). The Player King is sceptical but again his wife affirms, on pain of punishment, the sentiments that Hamlet cannot forgive his mother for violating.

Hamlet asks Gertrude's opinion of the play. Her famous rebuff 'The lady doth protest too much, methinks' (line 211) reveals she is aware that her son is trying to make her feel uncomfortable. The second half of the play presents the assassination in the garden, which

CHECK THE FILM

Most films and stage productions make huge cuts at this point. Some scrap the dumb show entirely. Most prune severely *The Murder of Gonzago*. Watch as many different versions of the play-within-the-play as possible, noting how different directors present the following things and how this shapes our understanding of the action. Is the dumb show watched by everyone? Is it clear what it means? How do Ophelia, Gertrude, Claudius, and the rest of the courtiers react a) to *The Murder of Gonzago* and b) to Hamlet's taunts? How convinced is Horatio that Hamlet's trick has worked?

Hamlet said he hoped would provoke Claudius into revealing his sins. But in Hamlet's running commentary on the play, he announces that the murderer, Lucianus, is not the king's brother, but his nephew. As the performance proceeds with no obvious response from Claudius, Hamlet becomes increasingly agitated, interrupting more and more determinedly until his final outburst: 'A poisons him i'th'garden for's estate … You shall see anon how the murderer gets the love of Gonzago's wife' (lines 237ff). This is a desperate attempt to provoke a response from a man who has his conscience, in public at least, absolutely under control.

When the performance breaks up, Hamlet is euphoric and convinced Claudius's conscience has been touched: 'I'll take the ghost's word for a thousand pound' (line 260). But Horatio's judgement is guarded and he is critical of Hamlet's performance. Significantly, Hamlet turns away from Horatio at this point to taunt Rosencrantz and Guildenstern and then Polonius. Guildenstern reports that the King is mad with anger, and that the Queen is 'in most great affliction of spirit' (line 282) and wishes to see him. To the spies, Hamlet explains his 'distemper' (line 305) as frustrated ambition: another message for Claudius's ears.

Hamlet is left alone on stage to contemplate what has happened as he prepares to face his mother.

COMMENTARY

In his advice to the actors and his declaration of his love for Horatio, Hamlet asserts the superiority of restraint and discretion over passion. He is saying exactly the opposite of what he said in his soliloquy in Act II Scene 2 where he was impressed by the actor's fervour.

When Claudius asks how Hamlet is doing, he uses the word 'fares' (line 82). In his answer, the Prince plays on this word, which can also mean 'eats'. He says he is like a chameleon, living on nothing but air. He is trying to make Claudius feel he is frustrated at not being the King. Claudius pretends not to understand him.

When Ophelia declares that the King has been dead for 'twice two

CHECK THE BOOK

For critical analyses of five film versions of the dumb show and *The Murder of Gonzago*, see essays by both Leigh Woods and David G. Hale in (eds.) Klein and Daphinoff *Hamlet on Screen* (1997).

months' (line 114), she is not necessarily being precise, but this detail confirms that there is a lapse of some weeks between Acts I and II. We are also reminded that it is not long since Gertrude was widowed.

The dumb show

Critics have been puzzled by the fact that Claudius and Gertrude seem unaffected by the dumb show. But Claudius is a man used to concealing his guilt. It is not that he is not affected by the show; it is that he does not *show* that he is affected. Gertrude has no reason to be upset by the mime because, as we learn in Act III Scene 4, she has no idea that her husband was murdered. The Player Queen responds to the poisoner's advances only after the Player King has died; common sense suggests that Gertrude and Claudius had been adulterous lovers long before King Hamlet died. The dumb show would convince Gertrude that the play was *not* about her.

The Murder of Gonzago

The play is in two parts; each serves a different function. During the interval between the parts, Claudius asks Hamlet what the play is called. He replies *The Mousetrap*. Later, in Act III Scene 4, line 184, 'mouse' is the nickname Hamlet imagines Claudius giving Gertrude. The first part of the play focuses on the Queen's behaviour before and after her husband's death. If Hamlet is out to catch anyone's conscience, it is his mother's he is after first, only then the King's. We are told in Act V that Hamlet is thirty. Pointedly, we hear that the Player King and Player Queen have been married thirty years. That detail would alert Gertrude to the play's having an ulterior purpose. What we have, presumably as a result of Hamlet's embellishments, is an indictment of Gertrude's infidelity to her first husband.

In some respects the second scene is another version of Hamlet's threat in the 'nunnery' episode, 'all but one shall live' (III.1.142); a clumsy warning to Claudius that his life is in danger. This is the second occasion on which Hamlet has had the word 'revenge' bellowed into Claudius's ear. It is as if he wants to provoke Claudius to act so he will not have to.

CHECK THE FILM

'The play within the play in Richardson's *Hamlet* presents Claudius as a red-nosed clown, Elsinore as a cardboard castle, the cuckolding of King Hamlet [as] a game of sexual leapfrog between the Queen of Hearts and her two royal studs and the murder as a festive dance around the Maypole turned grotesque as the King is strangled in the brightly coloured streamers and the self-crowned murderer leaps into the Queen's arms – its strengths and truth duplicating in terms of visual style the insane discord in Hamlet's mind.' Jack J. Jorgens, 'Realising Shakespeare on Film' in *New Casebooks, Shakespeare on Film*, ed. Robert Shaughnessy (1998).

CHECK THE FILM

The play has not proved Claudius's guilt; should we see, as Laurence Olivier's 1948 film suggests, courtiers looking at one another in horror as they realise their King is a regicide?

CONTEXT

The 'groundlings' (line 9) whom Hamlet refers to so dismissively, were members of the audience standing to watch the play in the cheapest part of the theatre.

CONTEXT

When advising the players, Hamlet speaks of overacting that 'out-Herods Herod' (line 11). Herod was presented in mystery plays as a loud-mouthed tyrant.

When Claudius rises it is unclear whether Hamlet's taunts or the play have unsettled him. As we hear later, it appears to the court that the King rises as a response to Hamlet's rudeness rather than because of anything sinister.

Polonius, Rosencrantz and Guildenstern, to say nothing of Gertrude, have blemishes in their characters. But they are not people who would knowingly associate themselves with a monster.

When Polonius changes his mind about the shape of the cloud 'camel … weasel … whale' (lines 340ff) it is difficult to imagine three creatures with less similar backs. Hamlet is ridiculing Polonius for being a 'yes-man'. Hamlet's euphoria becomes for a moment like the melodramatic language of Lucianus, the nephew about to murder his uncle: ''Tis now the very witching time of night … Now could I drink hot blood …' (lines 349ff). Yet his next move is not to pursue Claudius but to visit his mother. 'I will speak daggers to her, but use none' (line 357) – the cruel irony of which is that in her room he will kill Polonius.

GLOSSARY	
6	temperance moderation
9	are capable of understand only, respond only to
16	o'erstep not the modesty of nature act as if you were presenting real, not larger-than-life people
22	make the judicious grieve dismay people who appreciate good acting
28	journeymen unskilled workers
44	just balanced, honest, reliable, shrewd
48	revenue income
50	the candied tongue fawning flattery
50	lick absurd pomp Shakespeare often compares flatterers to dogs who slobber over their masters to get what they want
54	election choice (of friends)
59	commeddled balanced
70	occulted concealed
71	itself unkennel reveal itself, break out of where it is being kept

74	**Vulcan's stithy** the filthy workshop of Vulcan, the god of blacksmiths
77	**In censure of his seeming** to judge what we can tell from his looks
78	**steal aught** hides anything
80	**idle** behave as if I had nothing on my mind, or pretend to be mad
99–107	**shall I lie in your lap? … country matters … to lie between maids' legs … Nothing** Hamlet's crude abuse makes an impression on Ophelia; it surfaces in the bawdy of her songs in Act IV
122	**miching mallecho** dastardly deeds, sneaky villainy
123	**argument** plot
134	**brief … as woman's love** the theme of the first part of *The Mousetrap*
136	**Phoebus' cart** the sun-god's chariot
137	**Neptune's … ground** the sea and the earth. The language of the play-within-the-play is deliberately flowery, old-fashioned
138	**borrowed sheen** the moon borrows its light from the sun
140	**Hymen** the god of marriage
146	**distrust you** am worried about your health
155	**My operant powers their functions leave to do** a very roundabout way of saying 'I think I'm dying'
162	**wormwood** bitter
169	**Purpose is but the slave to memory** an ironic commentary on Hamlet's delayed revenge
200	**An anchor** a hermit, a religious recluse (perhaps in a nunnery)
211	**doth protest too much** is making too many grand promises, is being insincere
213	**argument** the theme of the play
219	**free souls** nothing on our consciences
220	**Let the galled jade wince, our withers are unwrung** it is only horses with saddle sores that flinch, our shoulders are healthy
226	**It would cost you … mine edge** Hamlet continues to punish Ophelia with gross sexual images

continued

CONTEXT

Shakespeare makes an in-joke for the Globe audience when he has Polonius say 'I did enact Julius Caesar' (line 91). The actor playing Polonius probably played the title role in *Julius Caesar*, being performed at about the same time as *Hamlet*. Shakespeare's version of the play was unusual in staging the assassination at the Capitol rather than in the forum.

CHECK THE BOOK

An illuminating examination of this scene, and many other complex moments in *Hamlet*, may be found in John Dover Wilson's book, *What Happens in Hamlet* (1935).

273	**marvellous distempered … with choler** Guildenstern interprets Claudius's mood as angry, not guilty
301	**were she ten times our mother** Gertrude is his mother twice over having married his stepfather
314–15	**drive me into a toil** trap me
324	**ventages** the holes the fingers cover to produce different notes
335	**you can fret me** (i) upset me (ii) mark me as a lute is marked to show where the fingers fall upon the strings
355	**Nero** the infamous Roman emperor who murdered his mother
359	**shent** rebuked for her sins

CONTEXT

Guildenstern and Rosencrantz, like Claudius's spin doctors, share between them a speech justifying in pious language whatever underhand things the King does to contain Hamlet in order to preserve the absolute power of the Crown upon which, they argue, the entire well-being of the state depends. It is an ideological statement which disciples of Machiavelli and monarchs who believed in the divine right of kings, would have applauded.

SCENE 3

- The King attempts to pray for forgiveness.
- Hamlet has Claudius at his mercy but cannot kill the King at prayer.

Rosencrantz, Guildenstern and Claudius are now united in viewing Hamlet as a threat to the crown – a danger that must be removed. The emotion perceived in Claudius's words and expression is 'fear' (line 8), not guilt. Polonius reminds us that he will be listening to the Prince's conversation with his mother.

Left alone on stage, the King attempts to pray, to repent of the murder. Passing through on his way to his mother's room, Hamlet comes upon the kneeling Claudius and recognises that he has an opportunity to kill him. He decides not to since, he reasons, if he kills his uncle at prayer Claudius will go to heaven not to hell. That would be poor revenge.

COMMENTARY

When Claudius speaks of 'fetters put about this fear' (line 25), the imagery of a prisoner's chains recalls Hamlet's description of

Denmark as a prison. The words are ironic; Fear cannot be shackled.

However, there is an eloquent dignity and sincerity in Claudius's troubled **soliloquy** that is quite different from the rhetorical hypocrisy that we have seen earlier. Claudius's soliloquy is unlike Hamlet's agitated introspections. There is no tension, no panic, no confusion. It is most like the steady-eyed despair that we hear in Macbeth's soliloquies in the final stage of his tragedy.

The dovetailing of Claudius's soliloquy with Hamlet's highlights the fact that, despite all his Machiavellian pragmatism, Claudius inhabits the same moral universe as his nephew.

> In the corrupted currents of this world
> Offence's gilded hand may shove by justice
> … But 'tis not so above
> There is no shuffling …
> Try what repentance can …
> Yet what can it when one cannot repent? (lines 57ff)

Despite his scepticism, this prayer saves Claudius's life, producing the richly ironic couplet which ends the episode: 'My words fly up, my thoughts remain below. / Words without thoughts never to heaven go' (lines 97–8).

Since Dr Johnson's famous remark that Hamlet's words here are 'too horrible to be read or to be uttered', critics have argued about why Hamlet spares Claudius. Hamlet's own explanation leaves few people satisfied. Each student of the play must consider whether Hamlet gives his true reason, simply rationalises a tendency to procrastinate or provides the sort of justification which might satisfy the revenge-hungry father who is haunting him. Or does Hamlet know that to kill a man at prayer in a chapel is cold-blooded murder and damnable?

Alternatively, we may remember that without Hamlet's delay, the play would be over very quickly.

 CHECK THE NET

Read what the eighteenth-century critic Dr Johnson felt about Hamlet's sentiments. You will find his commentary on *Hamlet* at **http:// shakespearean. org.uk.** Why might a modern reader react differently?

In fact, Hamlet does finally kill Claudius when he is 'about some act / That has no relish of salvation in't' (lines 91–2). We can only assume that whilst 'flights of angels sing' Hamlet to his rest (V.2.339), Claudius's feet 'kick at heaven' (line 93).

GLOSSARY		
13	noyance	harm
14	weal	health
15	cess of majesty	a king's death or overthrow
17	a massy wheel	a confused image of the Wheel of Fortune
22	boisterous ruin	tumultuous crash
29	the process	everything that goes on
29	tax him home	give him a telling-off
34	I'll call upon you ere you go to bed	dramatic irony. He won't, he'll be dead
36	rank	foul, filthy, disgusting
38	can	can achieve
41	a man to double business bound	someone trying to move in two opposite directions at once
47	to confront the visage of offence	look sin in the face
49	forestallèd ere we come to fall	prevent us from committing sins
50	pardoned being down	to forgive us when we do sin
56	th'offence	the fruits of sin
58	Offence's gilded hand may shove by justice	rich men can buy their way out of trouble with the law
61	no shuffling	no cheating
68	limèd soul	birds used to be caught by people smearing sticky lime on the branches of trees
69	Make assay	give it a try
73	pat	easily, neatly
79	this is hire and salary, not revenge	this would be like carrying out a 'contract' killing, not avenging what was done to my father
80	grossly	before he had an opportunity to repent of his sins
82	audit	his account in heaven
88	hent	occasion, opportunity

CONTEXT

'The primal eldest curse … A brother's murder' (line 37) refers to the first murder recorded in the Bible, that by Cain of his brother Abel.

SCENE 4

- Polonius prepares to eavesdrop on Gertrude and Hamlet's conversation.
- Hamlet kills Polonius believing him to be the King.
- Hamlet chastises his mother.
- The Ghost intervenes and whets Hamlet's **'almost blunted purpose'**.
- Gertrude promises not to reveal Hamlet's plans.

Shakespeare sets this scene in Gertrude's 'closet' (III.3.27), her private apartment. After instructing the Queen to behave like a righteous parent, Polonius again hides behind an arras. Gertrude attempts to chide Hamlet for his bad behaviour but he insists on questioning her about hers. Frightened by his manner, she calls for help. Hearing Polonius cry out, Hamlet stabs him, believing him to be the King.

From the shocked way she responds to the accusation, we discover that Gertrude did not know her husband had been murdered. Finally alone with his mother, Hamlet accuses her of gross sexual misconduct. He forces her to look at two pictures, one of the god-like King Hamlet and another of Claudius whom Hamlet compares to a mildewed ear of corn. Hamlet's distress is that a mature woman can allow her sexuality to have such power over her 'judgement' (line 70).

Her son's vehemence succeeds in breaking down the front with which Gertrude has suppressed her guilty feelings hitherto. She confesses that when she looks into her soul she sees 'such black and grainèd spots / As will not leave their tinct' (lines 90–1).

But Hamlet continues his passionate denunciation of her and is halted only when the Ghost reappears to spur on his revenge. Seeing nothing herself, Gertrude believes her son is mad, talking to thin air. Hamlet convinces her of his sanity and confides in her his suspicions about Rosencrantz and Guildenstern and the proposed voyage to England.

> **CONTEXT**
>
> The words **'this picture and … this'** (line 53) are a stage direction. In many productions Hamlet and his mother each have miniature paintings of the **'two brothers'** (line 54), King Hamlet and Claudius respectively, worn in lockets around their necks.

He says that he will 'answer' (line 177) to God for the murder of Polonius, but he is oddly untroubled by it. He feels Polonius brought his death upon himself. As in the 'nunnery' episode (Act III Scene 1), Hamlet seems to leave only to return to renew his attack. Having begged his mother to confess, repent and abstain from further sin, he tests his mother's change of heart, playing devil's advocate: 'Let the bloat king tempt you again … Make you to ravel all this matter out / That I essentially am not in madness / But mad in craft' (lines 183ff). But Gertrude has a new resolution and promises to reveal nothing to her husband.

COMMENTARY

The 'closet scene' is one of the dramatic climaxes of the play. It is the only time we see mother and son alone together. Apart from a brief exchange during *The Mousetrap* this is the first conversation they have had since Act I Scene 2.

The scene begins as a rerun of the 'nunnery' episode (Act III Scene 1): Polonius, eavesdropping, Gertrude speaking to her son with constrained formality, refusing to communicate. As before with Ophelia, Hamlet comes face to face with somebody performing, somebody to whom he was once close but from whom he has been deliberately separated.

Whatever ideas Gertrude has in agreeing to reprimand her son, the control of the interview is seized by Hamlet. He deliberately mocks the rhythm and the words of her reprimands, turning the finger of accusation from his own behaviour to his mother's:

GERTRUDE: Hamlet, thou hast thy father much offended.
HAMLET: Mother, you have my father much offended.
GERTRUDE: Come, come you answer with an idle tongue.
HAMLET: Go, go, you question with a wicked tongue.

(lines 9–12)

Where Hamlet has no appetite for revenge, this interview, like the one with Ophelia, serves a purpose that he cares about passionately. He is much more committed to saving a soul than to carrying out an execution. He can be 'cruel only to be kind' (line 179).

The interruption of their conference by Polonius's murder is curious. Hamlet's spontaneous, bloody reaction, 'Dead for a ducat … is it the king?' (line 23ff), is a dramatic contrast to his declining to take Claudius's life just a few minutes earlier.

The chief effect of Polonius's murder is to clarify the extent of Gertrude's sins. Accused by her of a 'bloody deed' (line 27) Hamlet throws back the phrase at her and retorts in a jeering couplet: 'A bloody deed? Almost as bad, good mother, / As kill a king and marry with his brother' (lines 28–9).

Gertrude's shocked echo 'As kill a king?' (line 29) and the 'wringing of [her] hands' (line 34) signal not only her innocence of the deed, but her shock in discovering that her new husband murdered her first.

There follows now an episode of passionate intimacy unlike any other in the play. Many twentieth-century productions have given the encounter Freudian overtones. But Hamlet's passion is more that of the zealous preacher than a would-be Oedipus. He sees himself as heaven's 'scourge and minister' (line 176). His speeches are peppered with the terms a confessor might use: 'for love of grace … Confess yourself to heaven … Repent … virtue … vice … devil … angel … Refrain … abstinence … And when you are desirous to be blessed / I'll blessing beg of you' (lines 145ff).

The Ghost's second visit, this time not 'in complete steel' (I.4.52) but 'in his habit as he lived' (line 136) establishes delay as a fact. Hamlet accuses himself before the Ghost confirms that he has let time slip (lines 105–10). Gertrude's graphic description of her son's terror (lines 118–23) is full of maternal concern and tenderness.

By the end of the scene, a new intimacy is established between mother and son which carries them into the final stages of the tragedy. Just before she dies, Gertrude will again mop her son's brows.

CONTEXT

An Elizabethan would understand 'closet' to mean 'private room'. In the twentieth century, prompted by reductivist Freudian readings of *Hamlet*, notably Ernst Jones' notorious essay 'Hamlet and Oedipus', there was a fashion for playing this episode as a bedroom scene, suggesting that Hamlet's feelings for his mother had sexual overtones.

 CHECK THE FILM

See how in his 1948 film Olivier presents this scene to suggest Hamlet's Oedipal fixation with his mother. For an analysis of Olivier's film of *Hamlet*, see Peter S. Donaldson's essay 'Olivier, Hamlet and Freud' in *New Casebooks: Shakespeare on Film*, ed. Robert Shaughnessy (1998).

GLOSSARY

4	**I'll silence me** dramatic irony. Polonius's shouts bring about his death
14	**by the rood** by Christ's cross
24	**Dead for a ducat** 'I bet you a ducat I killed it'
32	**I took thee for thy better** I thought you were the King
38	**proof and bulwark against sense** so hardened that it can no longer feel anything
40	**Such an act** incestuous adultery
41	**blurs the grace and blush of modesty** makes it difficult for people to believe anyone is pure
45	**As false as dicers' oaths** as meaningless as the sorts of things people promise when they're gambling
45	**Oh such a deed … A rhapsody of words** takes the spirit out of the marriage ceremony and reduces the vows the couple makes to nothing but so many pretty-sounding, but meaningless phrases
49	**Yea this solidity … at the act** Hamlet imagines the whole earth looking sad and so distressed by Gertrude's behaviour that you'd think the Day of Judgement was coming
52	**the index** an indication of what's to come (usually the contents page of a book)
64–5	**like a mildewed ear / Blasting his wholesome brother** although this image is Biblical (see Genesis 41) and the ear concerned is an ear of mildewed wheat which corrupts a healthy one, it is difficult to hear this line and not recall the Ghost's description of his hideous death
74–6	**sense to ecstasy was ne'er so thralled … in such a difference** the five senses could never be so controlled by madness that they could not tell apart two men so completely different from one another
77	**cozened** cheated
77	**at hoodman-blind** in a game of blind-man's buff
81	**mope** make such a terrible error
82–8	**Rebellious hell … panders will** If the devil can corrupt someone of your age, how can young people be expected to behave decently? There is no such thing as shame left when the judgement conspires with the appetite
99	**a cutpurse** the Elizabethan equivalent of a pickpocket

102	of shreds and patches more like an comic actor playing the role than a real king
106	tardy sluggish, lazy
106	whet sharpen
116	vacancy thin air
120	like life in excrements as if your hair were alive
136	in his habit as he lived the Ghost is no longer dressed in armour but in his everyday clothes
138	coinage of your brain … bodiless creation fantasy, delusion
139	ecstasy madness
145	gambol from refuse to do, run away from
145	for love of grace if you hope for God's forgiveness
157	cleft my heart in twain cut my heart in two
169	use almost can change the stamp of nature practice and persistence can almost change tendencies we were born with
176	I must be their scourge and minister Hamlet sees himself as God's agent punishing the wicked and helping them to repent
180	worse remains behind there are even worse things ahead
180	wanton lecherously

CONTEXT

The obscure image 'Unpeg the basket …' (lines 194–7) seems to be an allusion to a story about an ape that stole a basket full of birds which it opened on the roof of a house. When the birds flew away, the ape climbed into the basket and tried to copy the birds. Instead of flying free, it fell and broke its neck. Hamlet is warning Gertrude not to let his secret out of the bag lest she suffer the ape's fate.

ACT IV

SCENE 1

- Gertrude informs Claudius of Polonius's murder.
- Claudius decides that Hamlet should be sent away to England.

Claudius asks Gertrude to 'translate' (line 2) her sobs. She tells Claudius that 'in [his] brainish apprehension' (line 11) Hamlet has killed Polonius. Claudius maintains that 'this mad young man' (line 19) is a danger to everyone and must be shipped off to England next morning. He sends Rosencrantz and Guildenstern to locate Hamlet and to recover Polonius's body.

 CHECK THE BOOK

See what T. S. Eliot says about Hamlet's disgust with Gertrude in his essay on *Hamlet*, first published in 1919. For a new historicist reading of the closet scene, see Lisa Jardine 'What Happens in *Hamlet*?' in *Reading Shakespeare Historically* (1996).

CHECK THE BOOK

'Though Gertrude is still nominally the wife of Claudius, she is no longer, psychically or sexually, in dyadic union with him. She has ... consented to rejoin Hamlet in the paternal triangle, thus re-establishing the family configuration in its original form, prior to the intervention of Claudius.' John Russell, *Hamlet and Narcissus* (1995).

See the **Extended commentary** on **Text 2** for a detailed commentary on this scene.

GLOSSARY	
2	translate explain what they mean, what has upset you
4	Bestow this place on us leave us alone
11	brainish apprehension mad delusion
13	us ... we me ... I
16	answered explained to the public
17	providence foresight, care of this dangerous person
18	out of haunt under guard
23	pith of life my own life, life itself
29	The sun no sooner shall the mountains touch a poetic description of sunrise. It is after one a.m. (the Ghost's usual time for appearing) when this scene takes place
32	countenance take the blame for
38	our wisest friends we have no idea who these people are. Claudius's only counsellor was Polonius

SCENES 2–3

- Hamlet has hidden Polonius's body.
- Claudius confronts Hamlet.
- Once alone, Claudius reveals his plans to kill the Prince.

Rosencrantz and Guildenstern discover Hamlet who has hidden Polonius's body. He leads them on a chase.

Public opinion is beginning to ferment. Claudius explains that he cannot put Hamlet on trial because he is so popular. Rosencrantz and Guildenstern bring Hamlet to the King. The Prince taunts his uncle and eventually tells him where Polonius's body will be found. Claudius tells Hamlet he is being sent to England for his 'especial safety ... With fiery quickness' (Scene 3, line 37); he can scarcely restrain himself from telling his nephew what is waiting for him at the end of his voyage. We sense that Claudius and Hamlet are playing a game with each other. Hamlet bids Claudius farewell as his 'mother' (Scene 3, lines 46 and 48).

Alone on stage, Claudius reveals to the audience that he is sending Hamlet to his death.

COMMENTARY

These rapidly moving episodes are full of black comedy, generated by the two central protagonists, Hamlet and Claudius, pitting their wits against one another. Out of their depth, Rosencrantz and Guildenstern look on in bewilderment.

Under the licence of 'madness' , Hamlet plays the satirical fool. First he mocks Rosencrantz much as he ridiculed Polonius when he called him a fishmonger: 'Take you me for a sponge, my lord? ... I understand you not' (Scene 2, lines 12ff).

Shakespeare begins to polarise the virtuous and vicious characters as he moves the play towards its dramatic climax. He starts to simplify Claudius as the villain of the piece, Hamlet as the hero, 'loved of the distracted multitude' (Scene 3, line 4), so that in Act V we will be in no doubt where our sympathies are supposed to lie.

Hamlet's ludicrous leave-taking of Claudius as his 'dear mother' (Scene 3, line 46) is a curious anticipation of the farewell the crazy Ophelia will bid the King in Act IV Scene 5, line 71.

> **CONTEXT**
>
> Hamlet's words 'A certain convocation of politic worms' (line 20) are a second topical allusion to the Protestant reformer Martin Luther (see I.2) who in 1521 defended his rejection of the Pope's authority in a convocation (conference) held at Worms in Germany. Luther's words 'my conscience is captive to the Word of God. I cannot and I will not recant anything, for to go against conscience is neither right nor safe. God help me. Amen' have the ringing certainty which might appeal to a Hamlet, searching as he is for heroic integrity.

> **GLOSSARY**
>
> | 1 | Safely stowed Hamlet has just hidden Polonius's corpse |
> |---|---|
> | 6 | with dust whereto 'tis kin where it belongs. In the burial service the priest buries the body with the words, 'dust to dust, ashes to ashes' |
> | 11 | counsel wordplay. Counsel can mean (i) advice (ii) knowledge |
> | 14 | sponge flatterer |
> | 15 | the king's countenance the King's favours, his smiles and his money (on which the King's head would be stamped) |
> | | continued |

17	**like an ape in the corner of his jaw** like a bit of apple stuck between the teeth that is finally dislodged and eaten
21	**knavish** sarcastic
24	**The body … nothing** Hamlet confuses Rosencrantz by riddling about Polonius's and Claudius's bodies and which is where and what Claudius is worth
27	**Hide fox, and all after!** Hamlet runs off leading everyone on a wild chase
36–7	**th'offender's scourge is weighed / But never the offence** the public are more upset by the punishment than the crime that brought it about
39	**Deliberate pause** a decision carefully arrived at
32	**other place** Hamlet confidently expects Claudius to end up in hell
33	**nose him** smell his rotting body
41	**bark** ship
56	**cicatrice** the scar of a wound

CONTEXT

Claudius says that England 'Pays homage to us' (Scene 3, line 58). England was at that time forced to pay taxes (Danegeld) to Denmark.

SCENE 4

- Hamlet meets Fortinbras's army.
- Hamlet delivers his final soliloquy.

We meet young Fortinbras, leading his army across Denmark on its way to fight in Poland. We learn nothing more about him.

Hamlet asks the Captain of Fortinbras's army the purpose of their expedition. The Captain tells him they are fighting for a piece of worthless land. The Poles and Norwegians will fight for it simply to win 'honour' (line 56). Hamlet is disgusted.

Alone, Hamlet examines the action of Fortinbras and compares it with his own. As when he compared himself with the actor (Act II Scene 2) the comparison leaves him feeling ashamed. He resolves to have bloody thoughts from now on.

COMMENTARY

There is some evidence that Shakespeare decided to cut most of this scene as a result of his experiences of presenting *Hamlet* on the stage. The play is already Shakespeare's longest and, coming at such a late stage in the play, Hamlet's richest and most interesting soliloquy puts a considerable strain not only upon the actor playing Hamlet but also on the audience. If Shakespeare decided to cut these lines, therefore, it does not mean he thought them redundant or inferior to what he left; simply that, as drama, they were expendable. When we study *Hamlet* as a text, with plenty of time to examine the soliloquy closely, we may feel that what happens in Act IV Scene 4 is central to our reading of the whole work.

The episode with the Captain which precedes Hamlet's soliloquy is a powerful reminder to the audience and to Hamlet of his father's battle with King Fortinbras, which was similarly prompted merely by a desire for glory. Mention of the 'Polack' (line 23) recalls another of his father's famous victories (see Act I Scene 1). Hamlet's instinctive reaction on hearing that the Norwegians will fight simply for 'the name' (line 19) is contempt.

Hamlet's final, rich and complex soliloquy is cut from the Folio. It is also frequently omitted in productions because actors playing Hamlet, having been on stage for so long without a break, find its delivery exhausting. Audiences too are taxed by its intricate argument. However, it is the most revealing of all Hamlet's self-examinations. The soliloquy is the subject of detailed analysis in the **Extended commentary** on **Text 3**.

GLOSSARY		
2	by his licence	with his permission
22	A ranker rate, should it be sold in fee	a better price, if it were sold outright
27	imposthume	an abscess inside the body
32	inform against me	give evidence against me
34	market	use
		continued

CHECK THE BOOK

'Shakespeare has been remarkably skilful in his management of tone in the soliloquy as a means on the one hand of stressing again that Hamlet is a man of considerable intellect ... and on the other of revealing how the turbulent desire for revenge in him precludes dispassionate reasoning.' Alex Newell, *The Soliloquies in Hamlet* (1991).

CHECK THE FILM

When making his film of the play, Laurence Olivier cut this soliloquy, finding it impossible to deliver with any animation. Kenneth Branagh presents it with great gusto as the rousing conclusion to the first half of his 1996 film.

36–7	he that made us with such large discourse, / Looking before and after God gave us the capacity to reflect on what we have done and to weigh up what we should do
39	fust go stale
40	Bestial oblivion being like an animal, unaware of anything
40	craven scruple cowardly nit-picking
44	this thing avenging my father's murder
46	gross (i) large (ii) vile, disgusting
49	puffed inflated
50	Makes mouths … event makes scornful faces at whatever may threaten
53	an egg-shell something utterly worthless
63	Whereon the numbers cannot try the cause too small to accommodate the armies fighting for it
64	continent large enough

SCENE 5

- Ophelia has lost her wits.
- Laertes returns to avenge the murder of his father.

We hear of a girl who is 'distract' (line 2) and pitiable. Horatio advises Gertrude, in spite of her reluctance, to talk to her lest people start to have dangerous thoughts.

Alone for the only time in the play, Gertrude describes her soul as sick with sin and apprehension.

Ophelia comes in followed soon by Claudius. She sings confusedly about death and betrayal in love. Her madness is one of 'prettiness' (line 184) and pathos

The King is anxious. He tells Gertrude the people are uneasy, speculating about Polonius's death; Laertes has returned secretly from France.

CHECK THE FILM

In his film of *Hamlet*, Kenneth Branagh shows Ophelia being straitjacketed and hosed with cold water as, in the nineteenth century, madwomen often were.

A messenger describes the 'impiteous haste' (line 100) with which Laertes and his supporters, crying 'Laertes shall be king!' (lines 100ff), are advancing on the castle. Laertes bursts in, demanding to know how his father died.

Coolly, brazenly, Claudius rises to the challenge and promises to give Laertes a full account. Their conversation is interrupted by the second appearance of the mad Ophelia who comes in with herbs and flowers which she distributes to everyone. She sings a song about the death of a sweetheart and leaves.

COMMENTARY

As Shakespeare shapes his material in preparation for the tragic climax, the focus falls first upon Ophelia, then upon her brother. This scene is like a second exposition. A father is dead; we watch the ways his children respond. In Hamlet's absence, Shakespeare rapidly develops Polonius's children as stylised foils (contrasts) to two aspects of the Prince's personality. Ophelia's is a pitiably passive, Laertes' a rashly active response to the death of a father. Where Hamlet was melancholy and contemplated suicide, Ophelia simply goes mad and kills herself. Where Hamlet was instructed by the Ghost to undertake revenge and would not, Laertes plays the conventional revenge hero, free of all the ethical scruples which complicate Hamlet's performance in that role. The naivety and simplicity of their behaviour bring out the complex nature of Hamlet's.

Shakespeare lends dramatic variety to this stage of the play by using a young girl's plaintive music to generate pathos. Ophelia's songs are an affecting mixture of pretty sadness and bawdy. This recalls Hamlet's feelings in his bereavement where grief was mixed with sexual disgust. Also, with the words 'brands the harlot' (line 119) Shakespeare deliberately uses the same image Hamlet used when scourging his mother in Act III Scene 4.

Dramatic expediency explains why Horatio is involved here. He has nothing else to do while Hamlet is away yet Shakespeare needs him on hand for Hamlet's 'unexpected' return: there is no one else Hamlet could plausibly confide in so the audience could find out what had been going on at sea. But seeing Horatio and Gertrude

CHECK THE BOOK

'There is no sense in which Ophelia may be said to grow up in the course of the play', Maurice Charney, *Hamlet's Fictions* (1998).

CONTEXT

For a lady to have her hair down, as the First Quarto directs, 'Enter Ofelia playing on a lute, and her hair down, singing' (IV.5.14) would be regarded in Elizabethan times as an offence against social decorum similar to Hamlet's sudden appearance in Ophelia's closet (II.1.78–80).

CONTEXT

Claudius's hypocrisy in voicing the ideology of the divinity of kings when he himself has slaughtered the Lord's anointed marks him as the most Machiavellian of all Shakespearean monarchs. And for the moment, the bluster works!

communicating helps Shakespeare to continue the steady polarisation of sympathetic against unsympathetic characters which leads into the climax. This exchange between two people who are loyal to Hamlet is as symbolic as the conspiring of Claudius and Laertes against him which ensues.

The way Claudius outfaces Laertes reminds us of his air of bluff complacency in Act I Scene 2. That the man who killed his brother king can deliver the lines: 'There's such divinity doth hedge a king / That treason can but peep to what it would, / Acts little of his will' (lines 124ff) is testimony to Claudius's consummate hypocrisy.

Claudius's villainy is developed as we watch him begin systematically to corrupt the gullible Laertes. The rash young man quickly becomes a victim, tainted by what Claudius pours into his ear. His unthinking passion is no match for the sophisticated King's shrewdness and cunning. Ironically he is very promptly and effectively 'juggled with' (line 130).

GLOSSARY	
2	**importunate** determined, persistent
5	**hems** coughs as if she knows things she should not
6	**Spurns enviously at straws** gets upset by trivial things
6	**things in doubt** confusedly
9	**yawn … their own thoughts** read into her words what they want to believe
14	**strew** spread
15	**ill-breeding** trouble-making
18	**toy** little, trivial thing
19	**artless jealousy** natural anxiety, suspicion, fear
21	**beauteous** beautiful but the word reminds us of 'beautified'. There is nothing morally beautiful about the Danish monarchs
25	**cockle hat** a pilgrim's hat
38	**Larded** decorated
42	**good dild you** may God reward you

45	**conceit** thinking, grieving
50	**maid** virgin
53	**dupped** opened
58	**Gis** Jesus
61	**Cock** (i) God (ii) penis
62	**tumbled me** took my virginity
77	**single spies** one at a time
82	**greenly** foolishly, like a political novice
83	**in hugger-mugger** hastily, anyhow, secretly
89	**buzzers** gossips, scandalmongers
91	**of matter beggared** not knowing the facts of the case
92	**arraign** to charge with wrongdoing
95	**superfluous death** death many times over
97	**Swissers** Swiss guards, bodyguards
99	**overpeering of his list** overflowing the shores
100	**impitious** unstoppable, overwhelming
110	**counter** on the wrong track
120	**unsmirchèd** spotless, innocent, pure
121	**true** chaste
124	**There's such divinity doth hedge a king** kings are protected by God
134	**both the worlds** this life and the afterlife
134	**I give to negligence** I don't care what happens
147	**Repast** feed
161	**fine** refined
191	**poll** hair
197	**commune with** share
199	**your wisest friends** we never learn who these people are
201	**collateral** in conspiracy with someone else
202	**touched** guilty
209	**hatchment** coat of arms to show Polonius was a gentleman

CONTEXT

The plants mentioned are symbolic: fennel = flattery; columbines = adultery; rue = repentance; daisy = broken hearts; violets = fidelity.

SCENE 6

CONTEXT

Hamlet managed to jump ship 'in the grapple' (line 15). To make hand-to-hand fighting possible aboard ship, grappling irons were thrown to pull the boats side by side.

- Hamlet has escaped from the ship that was taking him to England.
- Hamlet asks Horatio to join him.

Horatio receives a letter from Hamlet, which he reads aloud for the audience's benefit. The ship carrying Hamlet, Rosencrantz and Guildenstern to England has been attacked by a pirate vessel. In hand-to-hand fighting, Hamlet boarded the pirate boat, which then broke free, leaving Rosencrantz and Guildenstern to continue on their voyage to England without their prisoner. The pirates treated Hamlet kindly in return for which Hamlet is to do them a favour. Hamlet asks Horatio to pass on more letters to the King and then to join him. Thus we are prepared to see them together at the opening of Act V.

COMMENTARY

Here we have more dramatic expediency: Shakespeare advancing the plot quickly at the cost of some credibility. Hamlet's letter describes a sequence of events which would otherwise occupy far too much stage time.

CHECK THE BOOK

'Although the play is filled with tragedy and horror, many of the scenes are extremely funny, and indeed for much of the action, Hamlet and Claudius stalk each other like two murderous clowns attempting to achieve strategic advantage over the other.' Michael D. Bristol, 'Carnival and the Carnivalesque in *Hamlet*', *New Casebooks: Shakespeare's Tragedies*, ed. Susan Zimmerman (1998).

A touch of the fabulous is introduced as we hear Horatio read Hamlet's letter describing his providential liberation from the ship taking him to his death. It contributes to the force of Hamlet's declaration in Act V Scene 2 that our destinies are shaped by God. Like his friends the actors, the pirates readily help Hamlet; he describes them as 'thieves of mercy' (line 17) and they seem to be part of the workings of a benevolent Providence. We never discover what 'good turn' (line 18) Hamlet is to do his rescuers and Shakespeare's attempt to make their charity seem credible is clumsy.

However, Hamlet is the only major character we see with 'the common touch'. He talks easily to the actors, the pirates, the sailors and the Gravedigger. It is plausible that, as Claudius says in the next scene, 'the general gender' love him (IV. 7. 18).

Hamlet urges Horatio to join him as he 'wouldst fly death' (line 20).

It is surprising to hear that Hamlet now feels life is preferable to death: we wonder what has effected such a change. It is also moving since we shall hear Claudius plotting to cut that life short in the next scene. The style of Hamlet's letter has a clarity and energy about it which reflects a new outlook in the writer.

Whether it be the sea, the working of Providence or simply Hamlet's escaping the stench of the prison of Denmark, the Hamlet we meet in the last Act will be in many ways a different person from the tortured young man we have been watching up to now.

CONTEXT

In Shakespeare's romance *The Tempest*, written at the end of his career, he uses a sea storm symbolically as a kind of baptism. Characters' old selves die and emerge sea-changed – the better for their immersion, their symbolic drowning.

GLOSSARY		
9	th'ambassador that was bound for England	Hamlet. He couldn't reveal his identity to the sailor
13–14	warlike appointment	threatening and heavily armed
15	put on a compelled valour	characteristically Hamlet responds energetically when others take the initiative
17	thieves of mercy	villains with kind hearts; the phrase recalls 'sisters of mercy' and 'angels of mercy'
21–2	too light for the bore of the matter	what Hamlet has to tell him is more than words can convey

SCENE 7

- In a letter, Hamlet informs Claudius of his return.
- Claudius and Laertes plot Hamlet's death.
- Gertrude describes Ophelia's death by drowning.

The King has been giving Laertes an account of Polonius's death. While we have been listening to Horatio reading Hamlet's letter, Claudius appears to have put his case to Laertes very effectively and has him eating from his hand. As he is in the process of describing to Laertes how he has solved the Hamlet problem, a letter arrives from the Prince telling him that he has returned to Denmark 'naked' and 'alone' (lines 43–51). Once again, Hamlet is tempting Claudius to take the initiative. Claudius speaks of Gertrude's affection for her

CONTEXT

Claudius uses astrological imagery to describe his relationship with Gertrude: 'as the star moves not but in his sphere, I could not but by her' (line 15). The medieval astronomers believed that each planet was moved by its own spherical force-field.

CONTEXT

We have seen how Hamlet's Christian scruples have instinctively prevented him acting upon his father's Roman injunction to take revenge. No starker contrast can be imagined between Hamlet's inability to kill Claudius at prayer (III.3 is often set in a chapel) and the hot-blooded Laertes' words here. Even Claudius is taken aback.

son: 'The queen his mother / Lives almost by his looks' (lines 11–12). As further indication of the growing separateness between Claudius and Gertrude, the Queen is now amongst those Claudius will deliberately hoodwink: 'even his mother shall uncharge the practice / And call it accident' (lines 66–7). Together the King and Laertes hatch a treacherous plot to kill Hamlet.

Gertrude comes in and in an elaborate set piece describes Ophelia's drowning.

COMMENTARY

Shakespeare writes some of his most vigorous conversation in the first part of this scene. In some 150 lines, Shakespeare recapitulates the stages of a revenge play, this time with the role played by an uncomplicated rash young man who does not go through any of Hamlet's deliberations. In lines 19–24, Claudius uses two different metaphors to describe the difficulties he would have had if he had put Hamlet on trial. The people's fondness for the Prince would, like a spring which converts wooden things into stone, turn all his offences into virtues. And their breath shouting in favour of Hamlet would turn the proceedings against Claudius, just as weak arrows can be blown back at the person who fired them by a strong wind.

The most interesting part of a scene composed mainly of hasty plotting is a passage sometimes cut by directors anxious to spare the audience's fatigue (lines 106ff). As Hamlet did with Gertrude, Claudius plays devil's advocate, testing the resolution of his fiery accomplice. Claudius catechises the would-be revenge hero, asking Laertes if his father was dear to him or whether in his grief he is 'like the painting of a sorrow / A face without a heart' (lines 107–8).

In lines 117–22, it is as if Claudius is aware of Hamlet's difficulties in keeping his promise to the Ghost. When Claudius ask Laertes what he would do to prove himself his father's son, there is a fine irony in Laertes' reply

LAERTES:	To cut his throat i'th'church
CLAUDIUS:	No place indeed should murder sanctuarize;
	Revenge should have no bounds. (lines 125ff)

Shakespeare continues to simplify and intensify Claudius's villainy by stressing Hamlet's contrasting virtue: 'He being remiss, / Most generous and free from all contriving' (lines 133–4) is a further nudge of the audience's sympathies.

Gertrude's much-anthologised account of Ophelia's death (lines 166ff) is one of several poetic set pieces in this play; a self-contained cameo in Shakespeare's earlier **lyrical** style. Many have commented upon its 'unreality'; it does not sound like Gertrude talking, and what she says she observed raises problem after problem. Her account is too sweet, too rich, too utterly improbable to fit either the situation or the narrator. But we have noted already Shakespeare's stylisation of Ophelia's response to her father's death and, given Gertrude's stated loyalty to her son, it could be argued that she sanitises Ophelia's suicide deliberately to spare Laertes' feelings and thus not add to Hamlet's danger. Gertrude deliberately blames everything in her surroundings for her death, rather than the girl herself.

This moment of **pathos** is followed immediately by the King's blatant lie to his wife: 'How much I had to do to calm his rage' (line 192). It completes the audience's alienation from the scheming Claudius and prepares for the pathos of Hamlet's death by treachery.

CONTEXT

Willow (see line 166) was an emblem associated with rejected, broken-hearted lovers. The lyrical qualities and dramatic appropriateness of this famous passage have been much debated. The speech has been widely anthologised and re-presented in numerous paintings and stories so that it has become a free-standing work of art in its own right. The English composer, Frank Bridge, re-presented it as a tone poem.

GLOSSARY

1	**Now must … seal** now you must see that I am wholly innocent
7	**so capital** deserving beheading. Dramatic irony: Laertes doesn't know Claudius has sent Hamlet to England to be executed
10	**unsinewed** not very substantial
17	**a public count** a public trial
18	**the general gender** the ordinary people
40	**Claudio** someone never mentioned again
49	**some abuse** a trick
61	**checking at** refusing to go on
63	**now ripe in my device** Claudius must be quick-thinking
66	**uncharge the practice** not accuse anyone of foul play
68	**the organ** the means by which you carry it out continued

75	Of the unworthiest siege of the least value. Claudius is a politician, which he thinks is superior to being a great swordsman like his brother
79	his sables and his weeds sober, rich but formal clothing
83–4	this gallant / Had witchcraft in't this fine fellow was like a wizard on horseback
86–7	As had he been … beast as if he and his horse were a single creature
88	in forgery of shapes and tricks in trying to describe his feats to you
94	made confession of you talked a lot about you
99	Th'escrimers masters of the art of fencing
104	play fence
111	passages of proof from experience
112	qualifies weakens
126	murder sanctuarize protect someone from being murdered if they deserve it
131	set a double varnish on the fame praise you even more than Lamond did
133–4	remiss … and free from all contriving trusting and incapable of treachery himself
135	peruse the foils examine the swords
138	Requite him pay him back
140	an unction of a mountebank an ointment from a quack doctor
142	cataplasm a plaster containing an antidote
143	simples medicinal herbs
150	our drift look through our scheme is detected
153	blast in proof fail to come off
159	A chalice for the nonce a cup of wine prepared especially for the occasion
166	askant leaning across
166	hoary grey-green
170	liberal foul-mouthed
173	envious sliver evil branch
177	lauds hymns
178	incapable of her own distress unaware of the danger she was in
182	lay song
191	douts extinguishes it

CONTEXT

A sword that is 'unbated' (line 137) is without the protective cap that was usually fixed on the point of the sword to prevent anyone getting hurt.

ACT V

SCENE 1

- Two Gravediggers discuss Ophelia's suicide.
- Hamlet and Horatio contemplate the mutability of all things.
- Ophelia's cortège arrives; Laertes' display of grief for Ophelia enrages Hamlet and the two men fight by her graveside.

In a comic episode, two Gravediggers discuss Ophelia's suicide and the impropriety of her being permitted a Christian burial. The first Gravedigger asserts the supremacy of his craft.

When his assistant goes off to fetch wine, the singing Gravedigger is approached by Hamlet and Horatio. After reflections on how death is the great leveller, Hamlet examines the skull of Yorrick, his father's jester and his own companion in childhood. Contemplating the jester's fate leads Hamlet to question the value of a great reputation such as that of Alexander or Caesar. Man is simply the 'quintessence of dust' (II.2.290).

A funeral procession approaches. The reduced ceremony indicates it is a suicide's body being buried. Laertes quarrels with the priest who refuses to profane the funeral service by doing more for his sister. Hamlet is shocked to realise it is Ophelia who has died.

Gertrude expresses her sadness that Ophelia and Hamlet did not marry: 'I thought thy bride-bed to have decked, sweet maid / And not t'have strewed thy grave' (lines 211–12). Laertes bids farewell to his sister in an undignified and theatrical way. His 'emphasis' (line 222) goads Hamlet to come out of hiding and mock his display; the two men fight by Ophelia's graveside. Hamlet declares that he loved Ophelia and sneers at Laertes' overblown manner. Horatio takes Hamlet off and Claudius uses the opportunity to urge Laertes on in the plot to kill Hamlet.

> **CONTEXT**
>
> The Church forbade suicides Christian funeral rites and burial in consecrated ground until the nineteenth century. They were usually buried at a crossroads with a stake through the body.

Commentary

This is one of the most important scenes in *Hamlet*. It defines the philosophical context in which the whole tragedy takes place. Throughout this play, taken from an old pagan story, the terms of reference have been Christian. All the major characters are aware of the idea that this life is succeeded by another in which divine judgement will come.

CHECK THE BOOK

With the words 'an act hath three branches' (lines 9–10) Shakespeare's clowns are making fun of a famous contemporary case of suicide. This is examined in the Arden edition of *Hamlet* edited by Harold Jenkins (1982).

Shakespeare's simple stage used the minimum of props. Yet the power of this scene is achieved largely by spectacle. It includes the most famous **tableau** in the whole of dramatic literature. The picture of the young Prince contemplating Yorrick's skull is a universally recognised icon. Shakespeare did not invent this memento mori (reminder of death), but he gave it powerful expression. The tragedy is that death will come to so young a person who has achieved a kind of wisdom as a result of his suffering; whom the audience has come to admire and, perhaps, identify with.

The singing Gravedigger makes a profound impact upon the audience and upon the Prince who encounters him. This disturbingly happy, anonymous sexton, singing and cracking jokes as he works, is amusing and terrifying because he is full of life and so at home with death. His daily trade is dealing with what most of us would rather not think about and struggle to make sense of. This is the man who has dug the grave in which Ophelia is to be buried. Soon he will deal with Hamlet, Laertes, with the King and the Queen. And finally he will deal with us all, whether we are Somebody or Nobody.

CONTEXT

With the words 'bore arms' (line 28) Shakespeare makes a pun. To 'bear arms' usually refers to a gentleman's coat of arms, such as Shakespeare had recently acquired. The joke is that Adam must have had arms (in the bodily sense) to be able to dig.

The Gravedigger is the great leveller's assistant; the holes he digs take us into the next world. Throughout the scene, Shakespeare plays with the idea of the Gravedigger as both an ordinary, funny, fallible human being who knows what is what at court and is not going to be duped, and also as some ageless, immortal, superhuman gravedigger to the whole world. His song is about the stages of human life that lead everyone inevitably to his rough, indiscriminate care. He refers familiarly to Adam and to the Day of Judgement. He has been there from the beginning of human history and will be busy until the final trumpet. Long before Alexander and Caesar, Claudius and Hamlet came into the world, the gravedigger was busy; he will be at his work long after their brief entrances and exits.

In their conversation, the Gravedigger reminds Hamlet of his father and the temporary heroic glory which the name Hamlet stood for. He began the job 'that day that our last King Hamlet o'ercame Fortinbras' (line 120). The Gravedigger has outlived both of them. His career in Denmark began the very day Hamlet was born and he will take care of him when he dies.

Yorrick, Old Hamlet's jester is twenty-three years dead and as Hamlet holds the skull of his childhood companion, all the jester's frivolity, vitality and energy are recalled to emphasise the nothingness he has become: 'Not one now, to mock your own grinning' (line 162). As he handles Yorrick's skull, surrounded by the bones of others, Hamlet sees everything in a wider perspective; he appreciates the ultimate insignificance of the man who at the beginning of the play he compared to a god:

HAMLET: Dost thou think Alexander looked o' this fashion in the earth?
HORATIO: And smelt so? Pah! …
HAMLET: Imperious Caesar, dead and turned to clay, Might stop a hole, to keep the wind away.

(lines 166ff)

In contemplating the fact that Alexander and Julius Caesar, warriors far greater than his father, are now no more than dust, Hamlet is exorcising the Ghost's hold over him. His scurrilous song marks a release from a burden of obligation to that awesome warrior whose 'commandment' (I.5.102) he has felt obliged to carry out but could not. If Caesar is ridiculously insignificant, his father becomes invisible. Later in the scene the Prince celebrates this emancipation by announcing: 'This is I, / Hamlet the Dane' (lines 224–5).

Finally he can claim the name as his own. In the next scene he uses the royal 'we' for the first and only time. This explains why in Act V Hamlet hardly mentions his father. He is no longer haunted by

> **CONTEXT**
> Hamlet's mention of Cain (line 65), biblical murderer of his brother Abel, reminds us of Claudius, who also murdered his brother.

> **CONTEXT**
> The skull is a special type of emblem known as a 'momento mori', a deliberate reminder that everyone while still sound in mind and body should take stock of his own life and prepare spiritually for the Day of Judgement.

CHECK THE BOOK

Political criticism points to the subversive nature of the comedy which opens the final Act of the play. The Gravedigger plays Hamlet at his own word games and outlives all the high-born characters he serves. Michael D. Bristol points out that 'Against the perspective of death and burial, all claims to hierarchical superiority are nullified, all the "serious" claims of economic, political or moral systems become the objects of laughter... In the grave-diggers' world-view, Doomsday is a horizon that corresponds to the overthrow of social inequality', '"Funeral Bak'd meats": Carnival and the Carnivalesque in *Hamlet*', reprinted in Susan Zimmerman (ed.), *New Casebooks, Shakespeare's Tragedies* (1998).

him; his failure to carry out the revenge fades into a wider view of justice and time. His experiences on board ship and now outside the castle confirm his intuition. To commit a deed on earth that would lead to eternal damnation would be madness.

Hamlet is a new man in Act V: there is a clarity, coherence and confidence about what he says which contrasts dramatically with the confused speaker of the soliloquy which ended Act IV Scene 4. In Act V there is no need for a soliloquy; Hamlet can share his most profound and intimate thoughts with Horatio.

GLOSSARY	
2	her own salvation the Gravedigger says 'salvation' meaning 'damnation'. A suicide would go to hell
10	Argal the Gravedigger is mispronouncing the Latin word 'ergo' which means 'therefore'
12	goodman delver fellow gravedigger
24	even-Christen fellow Christian
50	Yaughan we never discover who or where Yaughan is
57	a property of easiness something he is used to
58–9	the hand ... sense hands which do little work are more sensitive
65	jowls flings
67	one that would circumvent God somebody who thought he could cheat God
74	chopless with the bottom jaw missing
75	mazard skull
77	loggets skittles
86	sconce head
90	pate head
93	this box the coffin
115	absolute precise in his use of language
116	equivocation using words that can have more than one meaning
117	picked sophisticated
118	galls his kibe treads on his heels
140	pocky rotten with sexual diseases, falling to bits
146	a whoreson mad fellow a term of affectionate abuse

160	gibes jokes
167	Alexander Alexander the Great, perhaps the greatest soldier of all time and famous for his physical beauty
174	to consider too curiously to reason in an excessively subtle way
180	Imperious Caesar Julius Caesar, who conquered Britain
186	such maimèd rites very much reduced ceremony
193	obsequies funeral rites
194	warranty authority
194	doubtful suspicious, it looks as if she killed herself
197	the last trumpet the Day of Judgement; the end of human time
199	crants wreaths
200	maiden strewments flowers strewn on the grave of a virgin
209	liest howling suffering the torments of hell
215	ingenious sense fine sensitivity
228	splenitive hot-tempered. Not something we usually associate with Hamlet
243	eisel vinegar
245	outface me try to go one better than me
247	prate brag, rant
250	Ossa Greek mountain
254	When that her golden couplets are disclosed when her chicks are hatched

CONTEXT

In this scene, Shakespeare employs the sort of language that a lawyer might use: 'quiddities … quillets … cases … tenures … action of battery'. In particular, the legal jargon of 'statutes … recognizances … fines … double vouchers … recoveries … indentures' is associated with buying land and pursuing debts.

SCENE 2

- Whilst at sea, Hamlet sentenced Rosencrantz and Guildenstern to death.
- The King arranges a fencing match between Hamlet and Laertes.
- During the bout, Laertes scratches Hamlet with a poisoned sword and is in turn fatally wounded with it; Gertrude drinks from a poisoned cup, prepared by the King for Hamlet.

CHECK THE FILM

Shakespeare's script provides only the skeleton for the dramatic conclusion of *Hamlet*. Every production must make many decisions about how to stage the exciting climax, where action largely replaces talking as the dramatic focus of the play. For example, is Osric involved in Claudius's scheming or an impartial referee? Does Gertrude realise that she is drinking from a poisoned chalice when she defies Claudius or only afterwards? At what point does Hamlet know he is fatally wounded? How does the court react when Claudius is killed? How is Fortinbras's entry presented: as something cynical and sinister or as representing a fresh start for an unfortunate country?

- The dying Queen and Laertes accuse Claudius; Hamlet, knowing he is dying, takes his revenge and kills the King.
- Hamlet nominates Fortinbras as his successor and begs Horatio to tell his story 'aright'.
- Young Fortinbras orders a soldier's funeral for Hamlet and assumes power in Denmark.

Hamlet gives Horatio and the audience an account of his experiences at sea. Impulse, rashness and indiscretion led him to unseal Claudius's commission where he discovered the order for his execution. He shows the order to the incredulous Horatio. Finding himself in a 'play' (line 31) begun by others, Hamlet substituted for Claudius's 'a new commission' (line 32), ordering the execution of Rosencrantz and Guildenstern which he sealed with his father's signet ring he luckily had with him. This is the first benefit he has enjoyed of being his father's son. The next day came the battle with the pirates and the separation of the two ships. Horatio voices misgiving but Hamlet feels no regret for sending the two spies to their deaths. Since they '[made] love to this employment' (line 56) they are not on his conscience.

Hamlet's scruples about killing Claudius have gone: his way forward is clear. It is now just a matter of opportunity: 'The interim's mine' (line 73). His experiences at sea have convinced him that we live in a world supervised by a benign God and that He shapes our destinies, despite our clumsy attempts to do so. Crucially, he now sees it as damnable to allow Claudius to live and cause more harm to the country. Hamlet regrets the way he treated Laertes by Ophelia's grave because he can sympathise with a man who has lost his father.

They are approached by Osric, the King's man, who is an even more ridiculous version of the wordy Polonius. His verbal affectations and misprisions spark Hamlet into his wittiest moments in the play. Osric tells Hamlet that the King has proposed a fencing match between Laertes and himself. He has wagered that, in a dozen passes, Laertes will not beat Hamlet by more than three hits. Hamlet accepts the challenge.

Hamlet confesses to Horatio misgivings about the contest but refuses his offer to try and get it postponed. Death must come to us all one day; all that matters is being ready for it.

Claudius and the court assemble for the match. Hamlet apologises to Laertes, who accepts the apology but insists the match be played to restore his credit in the eyes of the world. The King promises Hamlet a fabulous pearl if he scores the first or second point. He drinks to Hamlet's success. Hamlet scores the first hit and Claudius drops the 'pearl' into a beaker for him. We realise he has poisoned the wine. Gertrude shows maternal affection for her son; she displays her loyalty by drinking to him, despite Claudius's attempt to prevent her: 'It is the poisoned cup. It is too late' (line 270) comments Claudius. His plan is falling apart.

Hamlet continues to out-fence Laertes and it is only treacherously, between bouts, that Laertes manages to scratch him with the poisoned blade. Hamlet is unaware of the trick and when, after a violent scuffle, the rapiers change hands and Laertes is struck with the poisoned foil, it is Laertes who reveals that he has fallen foul of his own treachery. The poison works quickly on the Queen and despite Claudius's attempts to disguise it, Gertrude proclaims the truth: the wine was poisoned. Hamlet orders the doors to be shut whilst the treachery is sought out. It is only after Laertes tells Hamlet he will die shortly – 'In thee there is not half an hour of life' (line 295) – and proclaims 'The king's to blame' (line 300) that Hamlet acts, wounding Claudius and then forcing him to drink from the poisoned chalice. Laertes and Hamlet forgive one another.

Hamlet's final act is to prevent Horatio committing suicide to join his friend. He begs Horatio to 'tell [his] story' (line 328) and, hearing the noise of Fortinbras's army approaching, nominates the Norwegian Prince the next King of Denmark. Hamlet's dying words are 'the rest is silence' (line 337). Horatio bids him farewell.

Fortinbras arrives at the same time as the English ambassadors who report that Rosencrantz and Guildenstern have been executed. Horatio prepares to explain to the 'yet unknowing world' (line 358)

CHECK THE BOOK

For Bertold Brecht's analysis of Act V, see *Brecht on Theatre*, tr. John Willett (1964).

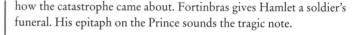

how the catastrophe came about. Fortinbras gives Hamlet a soldier's funeral. His epitaph on the Prince sounds the tragic note.

COMMENTARY

Hamlet's prose narrative to Horatio could not be more coherent or succinct. We see more of the consolidated world-view which accounts for the Prince's new-found sureness and optimism. The Hamlet who has returned to Denmark has a new philosophical strength. He has a grasp not only of his own situation but also of the universe in which he operates. Prompted by his heart and provoked by the treachery of others, Hamlet has learned that there are circumstances in which a person must act, not deliberate. In lines 63–70, Hamlet has reached a new moral position. He is discussing this calmly with Horatio, no longer passionately turning it over in his own mind. These lines contain four possessive pronouns – the cause is Hamlet's own, no longer a duty to a remote Ghost. By presenting young Hamlet as so witty and alive in the exchange with Osric, Shakespeare is preparing us for the grief we will feel when we lose our engaging hero.

His exchanges with Osric present in comically concentrated form the apotheosis of similar exchanges Hamlet has had throughout the play with those who abuse language and thus, he feels, the truth: 'To be honest ... is to be one man picked out of ten thousand' (II.2.180). Hamlet's sensitivity to the abuse of language was already apparent in Act I Scene 2, where he showed such hostility to Claudius calling him his 'son', and to Gertrude's unfortunate use of the words 'common' and 'seems'. For much of the play, it was Polonius whose inflated sense of his own importance and cynical abuse of his daughter led him to verbal quibbling and rhetorical excess (see 1.3 and II.2). Earlier in the play (IV.2.115–18) Hamlet commented that the Gravedigger's fondness for wordplay was symptomatic of the general decadence of the times and in his violent exchanges with Laertes (lines 214–59) it was Ophelia's brother's hyperbolic ranting which particularly disgusted Hamlet.

Now, as a dramatic foil to the climactic sword fight, the mood is closer to farce. Osric is an upstart courtier, 'spacious in the possession of dirt' (line 87), who has little to say but attempts to

CHECK THE BOOK

'Hamlet senses that he too has become part of a larger process: the plot of Providence as scripted by the divine Playwright.' James L. Calderwood, *To Be And Not To Be, Negation and Metadrama in Hamlet* (1983).

make a showy impression in his speech as in his ridiculous clothes by dressing up that little in as many words as possible. By the word 'impawned' (line 135) Osric means 'wagered' but this is obviously an affected way of saying it since Hamlet mocks him for using it; likewise Osric makes himself ridiculous by using the word 'carriages' (line 137). In his description of Laertes in particular (lines 101–5), Osric praises Laertes extravagantly and in the process misuses English ludicrously. Hamlet employs similar ornate terms, such as 'definement' (definition) and 'verity of extolment' (truth of praise), and thus **parodies** Osric in response. When Hamlet out-Osrics Osric, the courtier is completely floored by tautology, which for modern ears smacks of the Monty Python Parrot Sketch: 'Why do we wrap the gentleman in our more rawer breath?…What imports the nomination of this gentleman?' (lines 114–19).

As the plans for the fencing match are made and Hamlet senses chicanery afoot, he expresses most forcefully his faith in God: 'Not a whit. We defy augury. There is special providence in the fall of a sparrow' (lines 192ff). All that matters is being prepared for the next world:

> If it be now, 'tis not to come; if it be not to
> come, it will be now; if it be not now, yet it will come – the
> readiness is all.   (lines 193–5)

Many commentators have been unhappy about Hamlet's apology to Laertes (lines 198ff). Given Hamlet's evident sanity here and his scrupulous concern at all times for the truth, his laying of the blame for his behaviour in the graveyard on 'madness' (line 204), which he characterises as an alter ego, a false self, rings hollow. It is the Prince's most perplexing utterance. We have seen throughout the play that Hamlet's madness has been a convenient fiction, subscribed to for various reasons by Claudius, Gertrude and the Prince himself. Yet here, Shakespeare surely intends Hamlet to appear sincere? The tone of the final lines is moving. It is the reasoning that is unsatisfactory.

The dramatic qualities of the fencing match are not apparent on the page. What takes a few seconds to read may well account for several

CHECK THE FILM
Watch as many different productions of the final scene as possible, carefully noting what is cut, what is emphasised, what the directors and actors add in terms of stage business, music and lighting to generate the particular mood of the ending of the play.

CHECK THE BOOK

'Horatio's story is merely a bad quarto of Shakespeare's play, a pirated edition based on memorial reconstruction by an actor who, though he knows much, cannot possibly know all that has happened in the castle at Elsinore or on the stage of the Globe'. James L. Calderwood, *To Be And Not To Be, Negation and Metadrama in Hamlet* (1983).

minutes of stage time. After a play in which most of the activity has been intellectual, it comes as the latest of so many varied ingredients. Some productions show Hamlet realising he has been wounded and deliberately exchanging the foils and striking Laertes. This is not supported by the text, which generates far greater **pathos** by leaving Hamlet totally innocent of what is going on until Laertes tells him.

The Queen's loyal toast to Hamlet, drunk in defiance of her husband's command, completes the movement which has taken her from Claudius's side and restored her as Hamlet's loving mother. Whether she realises what she is doing or not is something each new production must decide, but the symbolism is clear. Finally, Claudius is isolated as the single villain of the piece, dying because of the accusations of the living, not as a result of what the Ghost told Hamlet.

Horatio's poignant farewell to his friend, 'Now cracks a noble heart. Good night, sweet Prince, / And flights of angels sing thee to thy rest' (lines 338–9), usually expresses the feelings of the audience. But when he describes the play in lines 359ff we need to ask whether his account leaves out anything central to our understanding of it. The audience has seen many things that Horatio has not.

In modern productions, there is often a note of irony introduced when Fortinbras gives the Prince so different from himself a soldier's funeral. His speech brings the tragedy to a dignified, exalted conclusion. But whether on reflection we feel Hamlet deserves Fortinbras's tribute, 'he was likely, had he been put on, / To have prov'd most royal' (lines 376–7) is the work of critical reflection. A pattern is completed. Young Fortinbras recovers the lands lost by his father to Old Hamlet and the throne of Denmark too.

CONTEXT

At sea, mutineers were punished by being put into iron shackles, hence 'mutines in the bilboes' (line 6).

GLOSSARY

15	**in fine** eventually, to cut a long tale short
20	**Larded** we can imagine the kind of oily language Claudius would use
23	**on the supervise** as soon as the letter was read
23	**no leisure bated** without delay

24	**stay** await
33	**statists** statesmen (Shakespeare had notoriously bad handwriting)
36	**yeoman's service** loyal service
38	**conjuration** command
43	**as-es** with a whole series of clauses beginning with the word 'as'; Hamlet compares them to a team of asses
43	**of great charge** heavily laden
47	**Not shriving time allowed** without the chance to confess their sins: the fate of Hamlet's father
48	**ordinant** helpful, in control
52	**Subscribed** signed
59	**insinuation** meddling in my affairs
61	**pass and fell incensèd points** thrust of deadly swords
66	**proper** own
67	**cozenage** deception
69	**canker of our nature** infection which threatens all
79	**the bravery of his grief** his showy display of grief
82	**this water-fly** Osric is probably flamboyantly dressed, so he reminds Hamlet of a dragonfly
86	**at the king's mess** the king's table
86	**chough** jackdaws chatter and imitate speech without understanding a word of what they are saying
87	**spacious in the possession of dirt** owns lots of land. But the word 'dirt' reminds us of the graveyard and how worthless all possessions are
114	**Concernancy** the reason
129	**imputation** reputation
130	**unfellowed** without equal
136	**poniards** small daggers
136	**assigns** accessories
136	**hangers** straps holding the sword
138	**of very liberal conceit** elegantly decorated
140	**edified by the margent** would have to consult the notes in the margin to understand what he was saying
142	**germane** appropriate
150	**vouchsafe the answer** a flowery way of saying 'accept the challenge' continued

CONTEXT

Sons did not automatically succeed their fathers in Denmark. Hamlet suggests that Claudius got himself chosen as King by devious means: 'Popped in between th'election and my hopes' (line 65).

CONTEXT

With the words 'there is special providence in the fall of a sparrow' (line 202) Hamlet recalls the words of Christ: 'Are not two sparrows sold for a farthing? And not one of them shall not fall to the ground without your Father' (Matthew 10:29).

Scene 2 continued

CONTEXT

There is a play on the word 'foil'. First, they will be fencing with foils (rapiers). Second, Hamlet says his own performance will be so poor that it will show off Laertes' skill – a foil is also a piece of dark material used to set off a jewel.

CONTEXT

In Classical Roman and Greek literature, suicide is presented not as a sin but as an heroic way for someone to end his/her life. Thus in Shakespeare's Roman works, Lucretia, Brutus and Cleopatra are praised for taking their own lives. By identifying with the 'ancient Roman' (line 323) Horatio seems to follow a different ethical code from Hamlet's Christian one. Yet a few lines later he calls on 'flights of angels' (line 342) to sing Hamlet to his rest.

154	**breathing time** the time when I usually take my exercise
164	**lapwing** young lapwings leave the nest soon after being hatched, sometimes still with the shell over their heads so they are unable to see where they are going
165	**comply with his dug** speak in an elegant way to his wet-nurse's nipple
166	**bevy** batch (of chicks)
166	**drossy** decadent
168	**yesty collection** a collection of frothy phrases
188	**gainsgiving** misgiving, intuitive sense of something being wrong
192	**we defy augury** I will not be intimidated by bad omens. This is the first time Hamlet has used the royal plural
202	**distraction** mental affliction
219	**reconcilement** reconciliation
222	**ungored** untarnished
235	**bettered** has the greater reputation
237	**a length** the same length
244	**union** a precious pearl. It's a showy gesture: pearls dissolve in wine. It is of course poison Claudius will drop into the goblet
264	**fat** sweaty
307	**tempered** prepared
315	**fell** terrifying
332	**o'ercrows** triumphs over me like a cock who has won a fight
336	**occurrents** what has happened
337	**solicited** – Hamlet doesn't complete the sentence
343	**quarry** heap of bodies of animals slaughtered in a hunt
343	**cries on** suggests
354	**so jump upon** exactly on cue
362	**forced cause** lies
369	**vantage** good fortune
377	**passage** music to accompany his funeral procession
378	**rite of war** a soldier's burial
381	**Becomes the field** is what you would expect on a battlefield

EXTENDED COMMENTARIES

TEXT 1 – I.2.1–76

CLAUDIUS: Though yet of Hamlet our dear brother's death
The memory be green, and that it us befitted
To bear our hearts in grief, and our whole kingdom
To be contracted in one brow of woe,
Yet so far hath discretion fought with nature   5
That we with wisest sorrow think on him,
Together with remembrance of ourselves.
Therefore our sometime sister, now our queen,
Th'imperial jointress to this warlike state,
Have we, as 'twere with a defeated joy,   10
With one auspicious and one dropping eye,
With mirth in funeral and with dirge in marriage,
In equal scale weighing delight and dole,
Taken to wife; nor have we herein barred
Your better wisdoms, which have freely gone   15
With this affair along – for all, our thanks.
Now follows that you know: young Fortinbras,
Holding a weak supposal of our worth,
Or thinking by our late dear brother's death
Our state to be disjoint and out of frame,   20
Colleaguèd with this dream of his advantage,
He hath not failed to pester us with message
Importing the surrender of those lands
Lost by his father, with all bands of law,
To our most valiant brother. So much for him.   25
Now for ourself and for this time of meeting
Thus much the business is: we have here writ
To Norway, uncle of young Fortinbras,
Who, impotent and bed-rid, scarcely hears
Of this his nephew's purpose, to suppress   30
His further gait herein, in that the levies,
The lists, and full proportions, are all made
Out of his subject; and we here dispatch
You, good Cornelius, and you, Voltemand,
For bearers of this greeting to old Norway,   35

QUESTION

'Bloody, bawdy villain! Remorseless, treacherous, lecherous, kindless villain!' (II.2. 554–5) Is this how you would sum up Claudius?

CONTEXT

The reference to 'one auspicious and one dropping eye' (line 11) would have made an Elizabethan audience think of the untrustworthy, two-faced goddess Fortune.

Giving you no further personal power
To business with the king, more than the scope
Of these dilated articles allow.
Farewell, and let your haste commend your duty.
CORNELIUS:
VOLTEMAND: } In that and all things will we show our duty.   40
CLAUDIUS: We doubt it nothing, heartily farewell.
[*Exeunt* VOLTEMAND *and* CORNELIUS]
And now Laertes, what's the news with you?
You told us of some suit, what is't Laertes?
You cannot speak of reason to the Dane
And lose your voice. What wouldst thou beg Laertes,   45
That shall not be my offer, not thy asking?
The head is not more native to the heart,
The hand more instrumental to the mouth,
Than is the throne of Denmark to thy father.
What wouldst thou have Laertes?   50
LAERTES: My dread lord,
Your leave and favour to return to France,
From whence though willingly I came to Denmark
To show my duty in your coronation,
Yet now I must confess, that duty done,
My thoughts and wishes bend again toward France,   55
And bow them to your gracious leave and pardon.
CLAUDIUS: Have you your father's leave? What says Polonius?
POLONIUS: He hath my lord wrung from me my slow leave
By laboursome petition, and at last
Upon his will I sealed my hard consent.   60
I do beseech you give him leave to go.
CLAUDIUS: Take thy fair hour Laertes, time be thine,
And thy best graces spend it at thy will.
But now my cousin Hamlet, and my son –
HAMLET: [*Aside*] A little more than kin, and less than kind.   65
CLAUDIUS: How is it that the clouds still hang on you?
HAMLET: Not so my lord, I am too much i'th'sun.
GERTRUDE: Good Hamlet cast thy nighted colour off,
And let thine eye look like a friend on Denmark.
Do not forever with thy vailèd lids   70
Seek for thy noble father in the dust.

CHECK THE BOOK

For a study of the significance of the verbal games being played in *Hamlet*, see M. M. Mahood's book *Shakespeare's Wordplay* (1957).

> Thou know'st 'tis common, all that lives must die,
> Passing through nature to eternity.
> HAMLET: Ay madam, it is common.
> GERTRUDE: If it be,
> Why seems it so particular with thee?   75
> HAMLET: Seems madam? nay it is, I know not seems.

A favourite Shakespearean theme is the discrepancy between appearance and reality. Claudius's opening speech appears relaxed, level-headed, eloquent and persuasive. But Shakespeare signals to the audience, long before they hear Claudius confess it, that the King's public mask conceals a troubled mind. The speech is so carefully structured that it is evidently rehearsed.

In the first two sentences, one point leads to the next with seemingly effortless poise, to be rounded off with a condescending flourish: 'Though … Yet … Therefore … nor … for all, our thanks.' Claudius sugars over the questionable marriage, carrying the court with him. Deliberately, he reminds everyone that until very recently Gertrude was his sister-in-law and is now his wife. It is as if he is testing the court to see if anyone dares breathe the word 'incest'. He pauses and, in many productions, receives at this point the polite applause his performance merits. Claudius deals with affairs in a businesslike way. Unlike his dead brother, the new King is a diplomat, not a warrior. He is confident enough to dismiss Fortinbras's 'holding a weak supposal of [his] worth' by voicing it as proof of the young man's folly.

If in using the royal plural so frequently, the new King sounds like someone trying to convince himself he is not a usurper, Claudius does not sound to the court like a man wracked by his conscience. The slave of a murderous ambition, he presents himself as someone whose judgement controls his passions. He says 'discretion' has overcome his natural grief for his 'dear brother'. Sensibly, he has balanced happiness and distress: 'In equal scale weighing delight and dole'. The **blank verse** flows and his sentiments sound plausible, until we ask ourselves whether emotions *can* be measured. Shakespeare gives Claudius just enough hollow phrases to alert the theatre audience to his hypocrisy. What is 'wisest sorrow'? How

> **CONTEXT**
>
> Claudius's eloquent, rational pragmatism immediately identifies him as belonging to a different mind-set from that of his old-fashioned warrior brother.

would 'defeated joy' feel? Can a person have 'one auspicious and one dropping eye' unless he is two-faced? Surely, 'mirth in funeral' and 'dirge in marriage' would be grotesque?

No one on stage asks these common-sense questions. The rhythm, the music of Claudius's verse carries him through. The imagery Shakespeare gives him tells us a different story.

In his stage-managed dealing with Laertes, the King parades a caring, indulgent self. He caresses Laertes, using his name four times in just nine lines. Happy to play the King's game, Laertes addresses him in appropriate language. Shrewdly, he refers not to the dead king's funeral, but to the new king's coronation as the reason he left France 'willingly'. In rewarding Laertes for his performance, Claudius is signalling to Hamlet that deference is what he demands. The exchange contrasts dramatically with what follows.

That Claudius deals with three items of business before confronting his black-suited nephew is another hint Shakespeare gives us that the King feels far uneasier than he seems to be. His comfortable control of affairs is abruptly checked by the Prince's cryptic but evident hostility. There is a striking discord between the steady rhythm and melodious tone of the blank verse we have been hearing and the Prince's witty and staccato responses. Unlike Laertes, Hamlet will not sing to Claudius's tune. His words are harsh and oblique. He speaks in riddles so that he can be rude to the clever Claudius whilst giving little away to the court. 'A little more than kin and less than kind' – Hamlet is 'more than kin' now he's both Claudius's nephew and his stepson. He is 'less than kind' in two senses of the word: he is neither kindly disposed towards his uncle, nor does he think he is of the same kind, meaning the same species.

> **CONTEXT**
>
> In the Renaissance, kings were often compared to the Sun. Hamlet later refers to his father as Hyperion, the Sun god.

They spar a second time. Hamlet continues to speak in a private language where a word has many different meanings: 'I am too much i'th'sun'. His uncle's fawning, calling him his 'son', revolts him. He is having too much of the 'son' and also of the 'Sun'. Shortly after this episode, Hamlet will express his longing for death, to be literally out of 'the sun'. As the proud son of King Hamlet, he will not submit to his uncle.

TEXT 2 – ACT 4, SCENE 1

CLAUDIUS: There's matter in these sighs, these profound heaves.
You must translate, 'tis fit we understand them.
Where is your son?
GERTRUDE: [Bestow this place on us a little while.]
[*Exeunt* ROSENCRANTZ *and* GUILDENSTERN]
Ah mine own lord, what have I seen tonight!   5
CLAUDIUS: What, Gertrude? How does Hamlet?
GERTRUDE: Mad as the sea and wind, when both contend
Which is the mightier. In his lawless fit,
Behind the arras hearing something stir,
Whips out his rapier, cries 'A rat, a rat!',   10
And in this brainish apprehension kills
The unseen good old man.
CLAUDIUS: Oh heavy deed!
It had been so with us had we been there.
His liberty is full of threats to all,
To you yourself, to us, to everyone.   15
Alas, how shall this bloody deed be answered?
It will be laid to us, whose providence
Should have kept short, restrained, and out of haunt,
This mad young man. But so much was our love,
We would not understand what was most fit,   20
But like the owner of a foul disease,
To keep it from divulging, let it feed
Even on the pith of life. Where is he gone?
GERTRUDE: To draw apart the body he hath killed,
O'er whom his very madness, like some ore   25
Among a mineral of metals base,
Shows itself pure; a weeps for what is done.
CLAUDIUS: Oh Gertrude, come away!
The sun no sooner shall the mountains touch
But we will ship him hence, and this vile deed   30
We must with all our majesty and skill
Both countenance and excuse. Ho, Guildenstern!
[*Enter* ROSENCRANTZ *and* GUILDENSTERN]
Friends both, go join you with some further aid.
Hamlet in madness hath Polonius slain,

CHECK THE BOOK

Kenneth S. Rothwell and Annabelle Henkin Melzer's *Shakespeare on Screen* (1990) describes eighty films, videos, documentaries and *Hamlet* derivatives, from Sarah Bernhardt's five-minute silent film of 1900 to Melvin Bragg's 1989 South Bank Show.

CHECK THE BOOK

In his *Eight Tragedies of Shakespeare, A Marxist Study* (1996) Victor Kiernen maintains that 'Gertrude seems too colourless a woman to be connected with anything as positive as murder.'

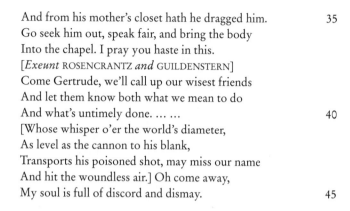

And from his mother's closet hath he dragged him.   35
Go seek him out, speak fair, and bring the body
Into the chapel. I pray you haste in this.
[*Exeunt* ROSENCRANTZ *and* GUILDENSTERN]
Come Gertrude, we'll call up our wisest friends
And let them know both what we mean to do
And what's untimely done.   40
[Whose whisper o'er the world's diameter,
As level as the cannon to his blank,
Transports his poisoned shot, may miss our name
And hit the woundless air.] Oh come away,
My soul is full of discord and dismay.   45

CHECK THE BOOK

'No one in this play "knows" or "understands" anyone else.' Linda Charnes, 'We were never early modern' in John J. Joughin (ed.), *Philosophical Shakespeares* (2000).

A powerful sound effect, Gertrude's sobbing, links Acts III and IV. As Claudius realises, 'There's matter in these sighs'. Yet the drama of this scene arises from Gertrude's refusing to 'translate' 'these profound heaves' accurately.

To help the audience 'translate' them, Shakespeare might have given Gertrude a **soliloquy** here. It would help us gauge exactly the effect the traumatic experiences of Act III Scene 4 have had on her. We have little sense of Gertrude as an individual or a very fully developed personality before the closet scene. Lacking a substantial soliloquy following it, we can judge her only by her behaviour.

This is the one intimate conversation between Claudius and Gertrude in the whole play. At all other moments, apart from their brief exchange in Act II Scene 2, conversations between Gertrude and Claudius are public. What they say is conditioned by the other people present.

What is remarkable about this moment of intimacy is that the couple share virtually nothing of what has just happened to each of them. Like his wife, Claudius is fresh from a painful moral crisis, explored in his soliloquy following *The Mousetrap*. He can share nothing of this with Gertrude. As far as he knows, she does not suspect that he murdered his brother. He signals a new separateness from her by referring to Hamlet as her son, no longer pretending that Hamlet is his. When at the end of the play he refers to Hamlet once more as

'Our son' (V.2.264) it is hypocritically, after he has prepared the poisoned wine for him. Shakespeare presents husband and wife as suffering in mutual isolation beneath a veneer of intimacy. They exchange words but not confidences. In fact, they tell each other lies.

Despite Hamlet's demonstration to her of his sanity a few minutes earlier, Gertrude develops the fiction that her son is: 'Mad as the sea and wind, when both contend / Which is the mightier'. She tells Claudius nothing about Hamlet's belief that his father was murdered or about his intentions to 'blow' his captors (and perhaps him too) 'at the moon'.

To justify sending him to England for everyone's safety, Claudius also pretends he still believes his nephew is a 'mad young man' whose 'liberty is full of threats to all, / To you yourself, to us, to everyone'. It suits the King's purpose to pretend that there could be neither rhyme nor reason in Hamlet's murder of Polonius. He acknowledges that 'it had been so with us had we been there' without exploring any possible reason Hamlet might have for wanting to kill him.

Claudius cannot share his fears of Hamlet as a potential **revenge hero** with Gertrude. If we believe what he says to Laertes later, 'The queen his mother / Lives almost by his looks' (IV.7.11–12), her affection for her son would make any plot to have him killed out of the question. Hamlet's behaviour must therefore be presented as irrational and indiscriminately dangerous. Gertrude dare not reveal to Claudius that Hamlet reacted with such coolness to Polonius's corpse, so we have the invention: 'a weeps for what is done'. She colludes with the idea that Hamlet is out of his mind and therefore not guilty of murder.

CHECK THE BOOK

For a study of *Hamlet* and the revenge conventions, see Eleanor Prosser's book *Hamlet and Revenge* (1967).

Claudius is uneasy for other reasons too. He cannot afford a scandal and does all he can to 'bear all smooth and even' (IV.3.7). With a shrewd eye on managing public opinion, he rehearses with all his 'majesty and skill' what sounds like a modern-day press release: 'so much was our love … Even on the pith of life'. The statement is as fluently hypocritical as his opening speech in Act I Scene 2. He is planning, after all, to send Hamlet to his death.

TEXT 3 – IV.4.32–66

QUESTION

Why, in your view, does Hamlet delay?

HAMLET: How all occasions do inform against me,
And spur my dull revenge! What is a man
If his chief good and market of his time
Be but to sleep and feed? A beast, no more.   35
Sure he that made us with such large discourse,
Looking before and after, gave us not
That capability and god-like reason
To fust in us unused. Now whether it be
Bestial oblivion, or some craven scruple   40
Of thinking too precisely on th'event –
A thought which quartered hath but one part wisdom
And ever three parts coward – I do not know
Why yet I live to say this thing's to do,
Sith I have cause, and will, and strength, and means   45
To do't. Examples gross as earth exhort me.
Witness this army of such mass and charge,
Led by a delicate and tender prince,
Whose spirit with divine ambition puffed
Makes mouths at the invisible event,   50
Exposing what is mortal and unsure
To all that fortune, death and danger dare,
Even for an egg-shell. Rightly to be great
Is not to stir without great argument,
But greatly to find quarrel in a straw   55
When honour's at the stake. How stand I then,
That have a father killed, a mother stained,
Excitements of my reason and my blood,
And let all sleep, while to my shame I see
The imminent death of twenty thousand men,   60
That for a fantasy and trick of fame
Go to their graves like beds, fight for a plot
Whereon the numbers cannot try the cause,
Which is not tomb enough and continent
To hide the slain. Oh from this time forth,   65
My thoughts be bloody or be nothing worth.

**CHECK
THE BOOK**

Character study is still alive and enterprising. Alexander Welsh in *Hamlet in His Modern Guises* (2001), explores the Prince as 'a distinctly modern hero' by comparing him to the protagonists of nineteenth- and twentieth-century novels by Goethe, Scott, Dickens, Melville and Joyce.

This **soliloquy** and the one in Act II Scene 2 have a similar emotional logic but here Shakespeare gives us a much more penetrating insight into the processes of Hamlet's tortured thinking. Again, he moves from self-disgust to resolving to act. His final words sound determined: 'Oh from this time forth, / My thoughts be bloody, or be nothing worth'. But this is ironic. As so often, Hamlet's actions contradict his words. His thoughts appear to move cogently to that bloodthirsty conclusion. But the speech is a mass of contradictions. It is the supreme example of Shakespeare showing that what someone *says* is not always what (s)he *believes*.

The speech begins with interesting imagery: 'How all occasions do inform against me'. Hamlet feels he is on trial; one occasion (event) after another comes in to give evidence against him. Who does he feel is his judge? The answer comes indirectly in the next image: 'And spur my dull revenge!'. He compares his revenge to a dull (spiritless) horse. No matter how much it is spurred, it will not get going. This interesting word recalls the Ghost's: 'And duller should'st thou be …' (I.5.32).

Hamlet goes on to try to define what separates man from animals. God gave humans reason and the duty to use it. Thinking, making moral choices is what distinguishes humans from beasts, makes us almost divine. We have seen Hamlet is what a person should be, a thinker, but now he asks whether his thinking is healthy. He cannot be charged with 'Bestial oblivion'. Does he have the opposite tendency: 'some craven scruple / Of thinking too precisely on th'event – / A thought which quartered hath but one part wisdom / And ever three parts coward'? To be a coward is surely to be less than a man? A man should fear nothing, shouldn't he?

But Shakespeare has gone to elaborate lengths in this play to show us there is not only life after death but divine punishment for those who sin. God-fearing men are good men, not bad. What can Hamlet make of this? That it is a son's duty to obey his earthly father because that is how things are in a pagan universe, or that he must remember that there is divine justice? Hamlet cannot articulate this problem; to do so would be to accuse his father of being a devil who asks his son, in the name of loving duty, to do what would cost him his soul.

CHECK THE BOOK

For two contrasting studies of *Hamlet* as a tragedy of character, see A. C. Bradley's *Shakespearean Tragedy* (1904) and L. C. Knights' *An Approach To Hamlet* (1960).

CHECK THE BOOK

'Hamlet talks far more than any other character in Shakespeare.' Sir Sidney Lee, *A Life of William Shakespeare* (1898).

So when Hamlet continues, 'I do not know / Why yet I live to say this thing's to do, / Sith I have cause, and will, and strength, and means / To do't', clearly this is not the case. He may have 'cause', the physical 'strength' and the 'means' to take revenge. What he does not have is the 'will'.

Hamlet proceeds to contract himself explicitly: 'Examples gross as earth exhort me'. This is illogical. The word 'gross' means 'foul, disgusting, savage, bad'. 'Exhort' means 'encourage, persuade, shove on'. A 'gross' example cannot exhort you to do anything except the opposite. Hamlet was instinctively sickened by what the Captain told him Fortinbras's army was about to do. Now, a few lines later, he seems to feel their behaviour exhorting him to do something similarly 'honourable', not in the Christian but in the pagan sense of the word.

QUESTION

'Wherever Hamlet looks, he sees reflections of himself'. Discuss and illustrate.

Hamlet completes his speech by rewriting what he has just seen. The passage raises many questions. Who is this 'delicate and tender prince'? Surely not the Fortinbras described by Horatio or the man we see? Hamlet is projecting himself into Fortinbras's situation, imagining himself playing the role his father would have wished him to play. What can the phrase 'divine ambition' possibly mean? Is it not a contradiction in terms? The cardinal Christian virtue is humility, not ambition. It can be seen as 'divine' only through pagan eyes where fame is the only kind of afterlife. What is most revealing is the repetition of the word 'straw' which Hamlet had used so contemptuously a few moments earlier. Here, he uses it in an attempt to justify the unjustifiable, equating greatness not with Christian virtue but with a concern for one's reputation. Somehow Hamlet has 'reasoned' himself into seeing the world upside down. He starts to sound very much like the hot-blooded Laertes.

Yet even as he does, we detect a false note. 'Fame' is, after all, 'a fantasy and a trick', a deceit. And who would fight for an 'egg-shell'?

PART THREE

CRITICAL APPROACHES

CHARACTERISATION

None of these characters is explored with the kind of attention to motivation and 'inner life' that Shakespeare expends on Hamlet and Claudius, whose characters are examined in the section on **The text**. Shakespeare's presentation of Gertrude is dealt with chiefly in the commentary on Act III Scene 4 and in the **Extended commentary** on **Text 2**.

POLONIUS

In Acts I–III, Polonius serves a number of dramatic purposes. In Act V some of these are taken over by Osric.

Polonius is the only significant member of Claudius's retinue. Shakespeare presents him as a man whose desire to serve the King is rooted as much in vanity and a sense of his own importance as in duty. The play shows parents controlling their children's lives. Like the Ghost, Polonius is an authoritarian father who demands unconditional obedience. But as well as presenting Polonius as authoritarian, Shakespeare also presents him as sordid. In Act I Scene 3, Polonius's objection to Hamlet's suit is that he has not offered a high enough price. In the scenes that follow, Shakespeare leaves us in no doubt about how we should see Polonius's abuse of his daughter. In Act II Scene 2 he says he will 'loose' (I.3.160) her to Hamlet, like live bait. There follows an unconscious pun on the word 'board'/'bawd' (I.3. 167) and it is at this point that Hamlet calls Polonius a 'fishmonger' (I.3.171) which, unlike the audience, the old man does not realise is Elizabethan slang for 'pimp'.

Polonius shows no interest in either of his children's views or feelings. Having given Laertes 'leave to go' (Act I Scene 2), a paternal blessing and a list of moral instructions to follow (Act I Scene 3), we see him sending a spy to Paris (Act II Scene 1) to try and catch him misbehaving. Twice he initiates surveillance on Hamlet. Eavesdropping finally costs him his life. Hamlet voices

CHECK THE BOOK

For a Jungian reading of Polonius's role as scapegoat, see Elizabeth Oakes, 'Polonius, The Man Behind the Arras', in Mark Thornton Burnett and John Manning (eds.) *New Essays on Hamlet* (1994).

Polonius's epitaph: 'Thou wretched, rash, intruding fool ... Thou find'st to be too busy is some danger' (III.4.31–3), the poetic justice of which no one in the play questions.

Shakespeare also uses the character of Polonius to parody Hamlet's habits: his love of wordplay and his tendency to 'think too precisely', 'to consider too curiously' (IV.4.41; V.1.174). Shakespeare generates rich comedy when Polonius regularly gets lost in tedious qualifications, elaborations and circumlocutions. We see this inclination in his first speech: '... wrung from me my slow leave / By laboursome petition' (I.2.58–9). The words lumber along, suggesting someone wordy and pompous. Later, , Shakespeare develops this affectation into a comic set piece: 'To expostulate ... I will be brief' (II.2.86ff). Polonius's drift getting lost in deviation and verbiage is funny in itself and contributes to the play's dramatic variety. But it is like Hamlet's own mental muddles and his liability to get lost in quibbles on the meanings of words, in self-expanding rhetorical patterns, unnecessary qualifications and speculations leading nowhere. Polonius is like a Hamlet gone senile, a comic version of the Prince's tragic sense of the complexity of things.

CHECK THE BOOK

An anonymous eighteenth-century critic (quoted in David Farley-Hills, 1998) said that 'To mix Comedy with Tragedy is breaking through the sacred Laws of Nature nor can it be defended'. Do you agree?

There is an element of Shakespearean self-criticism here too. In *Hamlet*, the playwright finds so many issues diverting that the progress of the play is continually compromised. When Gertrude demands from Polonius 'more matter with less art' (II.2.95) she could be criticising Shakespeare himself. Polonius's elaborate verbal decoration: 'tediousness the limbs and outward flourishes' (II.2.91) illustrate the very fault he is condemning. In his lines that follow, we see that Polonius is incorrigible.

Later in the same scene, Shakespeare also presents Polonius as a pedant: 'The best actors in the world, either for tragedy, comedy, history, pastoral, pastoral-comical, historical-pastoral, tragical-historical, tragical-comical-historical-pastoral ...' (lines 363ff). We can hear Shakespeare anticipating all those essays which will try to pigeon-hole this play, to reduce its rich dramatic variety to a formula.

LAERTES

Polonius's son is present in Act I Scene 2 and Act I Scene 3 then absent until half way through Act IV. When Polonius and then Ophelia pass out of the action, Laertes takes their place in the spotlight as a foil to Hamlet.

A striking contrast between Prince Hamlet and Laertes is established on their first appearance in the play; it is elaborated and developed in Acts IV and V when the revengeful Laertes first challenges the King and then becomes his accomplice in the plot that kills the Prince.

Laertes is more a set of attitudes than a psychologically elaborated character. In the final stages of the drama, he speaks and behaves as an uncomplicated **revenge hero**, explicitly brushing aside almost all the moral objections that have prevented Hamlet from playing the role. Shakespeare emphasises this dramatic function of Laertes when he has Hamlet say: 'For by the image of my cause, I see / The portraiture of his' (V.2.77–8).

Laertes' speeches in Act IV Scene 5 give us, in the starkest possible terms, the code, the creed of the revenge hero. For Laertes, no thought is required to arrive at this position. The sequence (IV.5.117–136) is a deliberate, point-by-point recapitulation of the stages of Hamlet's deliberations for the last four Acts, pruned of doubts, hesitation and qualifications.

Laertes resembles the Young Fortinbras described by Horatio in Act I Scene 1. He too is 'of unimprovèd mettle hot and full' (line 96). He lacks not only the Prince's Wittenberg education but also the mental equipment which Hamlet argued in his Act IV Scene 4 **soliloquy** distinguished a man from a beast. Shakespeare shows Laertes to be Polonius's son in the way he too abuses language. In place of his father's tedious elaborations, he gives Laertes a fondness for hyperbole and rant. Absurdly he compares himself to the 'life-rendering pelican' (IV.5.146). Pelicans were credited with giving their own blood to nourish their young.

QUESTION

Write an essay on the portrayal of the relationship between fathers and children in *Hamlet*.

CHECK THE BOOK

'Neither [Ophelia's] love nor her life really concerned [Laertes], nor does he trouble himself with the problematic nature of her death. All he cares for is a showy funeral.' Walter N. King, *Hamlet's Search for Meaning* (1982).

CHECK THE BOOK

'Laertes is not a whiff of fresh air. He is a hurricane. He rushes into the palace in an uncontrolled rage, roaring for blood, having no idea whom he seeks but ready "swoopstake", to smash all in his way. He defies his sovereign King, his conscience and his God. This is one of the most dreadful speeches in all Shakespeare, matched in its total surrender to malignant fury only by the terrible curses of Lear.' Eleanor Prosser, *Hamlet and Revenge* (1967).

Laertes is more concerned with appearances than reality as his description of his foolish and disreputable father as 'noble' (IV.7.25) underlines. He is upset not by his father's death but by his 'obscure funeral' (IV.5.208). It is the lack of 'formal ostentation' (IV.5.210) that grieves him because it reflects on his own standing in the eyes of the world. In Act IV Scene 7, lines 69ff, Claudius flatters Laertes, making much of Laertes' reputation, in order to make him malleable to his wicked plan.

In the graveyard scene, Shakespeare contrasts the simplicity of Hamlet's 'I loved Ophelia' (V.1.236) with her brother's verbose theatricality. Laertes' distress sounds simulated; his language is mannered, overdone and melodramatic. Again he is more upset by the lack of an impressive funeral than by bereavement. When he voices his anguish, the audience finds it affected. As part of his criticism of the abuse of language, Shakespeare has Laertes play a numbers game. He talks of 'tears seven times salt' (IV.5.154) and later he falls into the same habit: 'Oh treble woe / Fall ten times treble on that cursed head ...' (V.1.213ff). Straining for the effect of grandeur, the imagery of lines 218ff sounds hollow.

Incensed by this self-conscious display, Hamlet articulates the criticism of Laertes' language for us: 'What is he whose grief / Bears such an emphasis? whose phrase of sorrow / Conjures the wandering stars ...' (V.1.221–3). The Prince mocks Laertes' suggestion that grief can be expressed in quantitative terms: 'forty thousand brothers / Could not with all their quantity of love / Make up my sum' (V.1.236–8) and ridicules his love of hyperbole:

> Woo't weep, woo't fight, woo't fast, woo't tear thyself?
> Woo't drink up eisel, eat a crocodile? ...
> And if thou prate of mountains, let them throw
> Millions of acres on us, till our ground,
> Singeing his pate against the burning zone,
> Make Ossa like a wart. Nay, and thou'lt mouth,
> I'll rant as well as thou.
>
> (V.1.242–8)

Laertes is the instrument of Claudius's treachery in the exciting sword-fight which precipitates the final catastrophe. However,

Shakespeare includes Laertes in the reconciliation that unites him with Hamlet and Gertrude against the King. It is the young man's dying words, 'the king, the king's to blame' (V.2.300), that finally energise Hamlet's vengeance.

OPHELIA

'The fair Ophelia' is passive almost to the point of non-existence as an independent consciousness and is, to some extent, a more extreme version of Gertrude. She speaks to the King and Queen only when she is mad. Actresses have to struggle if they wish to inject a note of irony, archness or defiance into the few words she exchanges with brother, father or Hamlet. Shakespeare exploits this passivity to provoke responses from other characters in the play and from the audience.

When Hamlet delivers the judgement 'frailty thy name is woman' (I.2.146), he is unconsciously commenting upon both his mother and his girlfriend. Their behaviour is linked, this time deliberately, just before the performance of *The Mousetrap* when he comments on the short-lived nature of 'woman's love' (III.2.135).

In her uncomplicated obedience to her father, Ophelia is radically different from other young women in similar situations in Shakespearean plays. Juliet, Hermia, Desdemona, Cordelia, Perdita and Miranda, for example, all explicitly put their love for their prospective husbands before their obedience to fathers, defying far more intimidating figures than Polonius.

In Ophelia's case, there is not even a gesture of a struggle. Shakespeare does little to develop her. She is presented as someone with no point of view; as she says, 'I do not know my lord what I should think' (I.3.104). She promises twice to write to Laertes and perhaps her letters bring him home. She makes no attempt to communicate with Hamlet. There are two occasions when she could confide to him in whispers as perhaps he does to her. Shakespeare keeps her silent.

After the 'nunnery' episode (Act III Scene 1), Ophelia speaks to the audience for the only time in the play. She presents herself entirely

 CHECK THE BOOK
'Through madness, the women on stage can suddenly make a forceful assertion of their being. The lyric form and broken syntax and unbridled imagination all show ways of breaking through unbearable social restraints.' Maurice Charney, *Hamlet's Fictions* (1998).

QUESTION

'The relationship between Hamlet and Ophelia is ultimately a mystery – it remains frustratingly incomplete, undeveloped and contradictory.' Discuss your response to Shakespeare's depiction of the relationship between the couple in the light of this comment.

as the victim of Hamlet's rough treatment. There is no introspection, no sign that she feels she has behaved in any way shamefully. Nor does she express any understanding of Hamlet's pain. Her lament for the man he once was is generalised and conventional. At the point in the play when Claudius can hear that Hamlet is not mad, Ophelia describes him as 'Blasted with ecstasy' (III.1.154). She chooses to regard everything Hamlet has said to her as madness rather than consider whether her own behaviour has in any way provoked it.

By the end of Act IV and through into Act V, Ophelia achieves ultimate passivity and paradoxically a new kind of power, first in her distraction, then in the brook and finally in her coffin. Her incapacity, which has been a theme since Act I Scene 3, modulates into 'madness' (IV.5.156) presented as plaintive songs and pretty nonsense. This, together with Gertrude's stylised presentation of her death, offers decoration in place of any attempt at psychological elaboration. Her madness is less 'real' than Hamlet's confused states of mind because it is so tidy, unproblematic and unthreatening. She is presented as an innocent victim of other people's wickedness. Gertrude describes Ophelia's suicide as something involuntary. Interestingly, the Gravedigger is sceptical.

OSRIC

Appearing only in Act V, Osric assumes and develops some of the dramatic functions previously discharged by Polonius. When the King needs a courtier, Osric serves. He takes the news of the wager to Hamlet and presides over the fatal fencing match. There is nothing to suggest he is aware of the chicanery Claudius and Laertes are involved in. But in Act V Scene 2, lines 80–170, Shakespeare uses Osric to demonstrate the way in which the misuse of language reflects the moral degeneration of the kingdom.

ROSENCRANTZ AND GUILDENSTERN

The phrase 'Rosencrantz and Guildenstern' with its balanced trisyllabic names is reversible. It rolls off the tongue equally well either way round and, since we almost never see one of these characters without the other, directors who capitalise on the couple's lack of separate identities are doing no more than Shakespeare suggested. Often he divides a speech between them as if they are one character cut in two: 'Both your majesties ... to be commanded' (II.2.26–32).

With the popularity of Tom Stoppard's brilliant spoof, *Rosencrantz and Guildenstern Are Dead*, these two characters have been reinvented and today it is difficult to present them in the theatre other than as a pair of buffoons, a latter-day Tweedledum and Tweedledee. It has become a theatrical convention for the King, the Queen and even Rosencrantz and Guildenstern's old friend Hamlet to find it difficult to remember which character is which: 'Thanks Rosencrantz, and gentle Guildenstern. / Thanks Guildenstern, and gentle Rosencrantz' (II.2.33–4). While not diluting the sense of Hamlet as a victim of treachery, the incidental humour generated whenever the pair is on stage adds to the play's variety.

QUESTION

Examine the ways in which deception and scheming are woven into the dramatic structure of *Hamlet*.

Rosencrantz and Guildenstern are two characters caught up in an action too big for them. They lack the guile or ruthlessness to play the parts that Claudius has assigned to them. They give themselves away: 'there is a kind of confession in your looks which your modesties have not craft enough to colour' (II.2.265–6). Hirelings, they end up being destroyed by a plot within a plot of which they have no understanding and over which they have no control. Hamlet warns them off but they are either too greedy: 'Your visitation shall receive such thanks / As fits a king's remembrance' (II.2.25–6),

and

> ROSENCRANTZ: Take you me for a sponge my lord?
> HAMLET: Ay sir, that soaks up the king's countenance, his
> rewards   (V.2.14–15)

or too stupid to heed him.

To emphasise their lack of control over their fates, Shakespeare deliberately associates Rosencrantz and Guildenstern with the goddess Fortune and her ever-turning wheel. In their first meeting

CHECK THE FILM
The brilliantly witty *Rosencrantz and Guildenstern are Dead* (directed by Tom Stoppard and based on his play) re-presents certain episodes from Shakespeare's *Hamlet* as they might have been perceived and interpreted by these two minor characters, caught up in and confused by a plot over which they have no control.

with Hamlet, they joke about living in Fortune's 'privates' (II.2.225). Hamlet reminds them that Fortune is a 'strumpet' (II.2.227) and should not be relied upon. His language here and later in this episode underlines the parallel between Ophelia and Rosencrantz and Guildenstern, in that they all allow themselves to be used by the King against Hamlet.

In Act III Scene 3, when the pair are at their most sycophantic, Shakespeare gives Rosencrantz a speech ostensibly justifying whatever the King wishes to do. It contains an ironic warning to them both of their fate, were they perceptive enough to realise it: 'The cess of majesty … the boistrous ruin' (III.3.15–22). As the passage foreshadows, they will be destroyed in the first stage of the catastrophe which ends with Claudius's death. Their execution causes no great sadness in the audience. As Hamlet says: 'they did make love to this employment. / They are not near my conscience' (V. 2. 57–8).

HORATIO

Like Polonius, Horatio serves several important dramatic functions in the play. As the 'one man picked out of ten thousand' (II.2.176–7) who is honest, Shakespeare establishes him in Act I Scene 1 as a person the audience can trust. In his role as a **chorus**, the sceptical Horatio establishes the 'reality' of the Ghost and its close resemblance to Hamlet's father. He also sets the political scene.

As a character, Horatio is presented to us as utterly dependable, well educated, stoical, dispassionate and devout. Of all the major characters, he alone remains uncontaminated by the corruption in Elsinore, and Hamlet's election of him as the person to tell his story is thoroughly appropriate.

Horatio's friendship with Hamlet is one of the few unsullied beauties in the play. It is contrasted deliberately with Hamlet's relationships with Ophelia, Rosencrantz and Guildenstern, all of whom betray him.

Horatio has no biography beyond what the Prince tells us: 'But what in faith make you from Wittenberg? … fellow student'

(I.2.168ff), and 'no revenue hast but thy good spirits / To feed and clothe thee ... A man that Fortune's buffets and rewards / Hast ta'en with equal thanks' (III.2.46ff).

Horatio's words are few but the effect of them is the opposite of what we have with Ophelia. At critical moments he challenges, impartially, anything short of the truth. In Act I Scene 2, he will not permit Marcellus and Barnardo to exaggerate how long the Ghost's visit lasted. When *The Mousetrap* breaks up and Hamlet clearly wishes his friend to praise his stage management and confirm that Claudius's behaviour was suspicious, Horatio is scrupulously impartial. He will award Hamlet only 'Half a share' (III.2.254) in a company of players and when pressed about the King's demeanour says stubbornly, 'I did very well note him' (III.2.264). His words are neutral. Hamlet's turning away from him at this point to harry Rosencrantz and Guildenstern suggests Hamlet hears in them the truth he tries to deny.

Essentially static, Horatio expresses no affections save those revealed at the end for the Prince he bravely attempts to join in death.

At the beginning of the action, while everything seemed in a state of the greatest turmoil, Horatio expressed his faith: 'Heaven will direct it' (I.4.91). When, in the final scene, Hamlet voices the sentiment as his own, Horatio's affirmation is emphatic:

> HAMLET: There's a divinity that shapes our end
>   Rough-hew them how we will
> HORATIO: That is most certain   (V.2.10–12)

His fellow student at the university of Wittenberg, a centre of radical moral and religious philosophy, Horatio embodies many of the qualities Hamlet most admires. There is a Horatio-like side of Hamlet. It is as far removed from the **revenge hero** and the passionate man of action he envied in his **soliloquies** in Act II Scene 2 and Act IV Scene 4, as can be imagined. In Hamlet's most quiet, reflective and tender interlude (III.2.46ff), it is Horatio's qualities that the Prince celebrates: 'Give me that man / That is not passion's

CHECK THE BOOK

In an attempt to explain Hamlet's declaration of love to Horatio, a radical reading suggests that the Prince was a woman (P. Vining, *The Mystery of Hamlet. An Attempt to Solve An Old Problem*, 1881). Inspired by this idea was Asta Nielsen's silent film. It is discussed by Ann Thompson in 'Asta Nielsen and the Mystery of *Hamlet*' in Lynda E. Boose and Richard Burt (eds.) *Shakespeare the Movie* (1997).

slave, and I will wear him / In my heart's core, ay in my heart of heart, / As I do thee' (lines 61–4).

YOUNG FORTINBRAS

Complementing the way he presents Hamlet and Laertes as two very different characters playing the **revenge hero**'s role, Shakespeare presents the audience with two princes with radically different temperaments who find themselves in similar situations. Both kings gave their names to their sons and thus their warrior reputations to live up to.

CONTEXT

The names Fortinbras and Hamlet are historically linked. On the day Prince Hamlet was born, his father, King Hamlet, killed King Fortinbras in ceremonious single combat and was judged by the world a hero.

Young Fortinbras's aim in life is clear: 'to recover ... by strong hand / And terms compulsory those ... lands / So by his father lost' (I.1.102–4). Young Fortinbras, who is described by Horatio as 'of unimprovèd mettle hot and full' (II.1.96), seems to be following faithfully in his warrior father's footsteps, whereas young Hamlet has been at university in Wittenberg. Like King Hamlet, King Fortinbras has been succeeded as king not by his son but by his brother. The movements of both nephews are controlled by their uncles. In Act I Scene 2, Claudius writes to the King of Norway to suppress Young Fortinbras's threatened invasion of Denmark. When the Danish ambassadors return to announce that this has been accomplished (Act II Scene 2), we hear that Young Fortinbras will now lead his forces to wage a campaign in Poland instead, if Claudius will grant permission for the Norwegian forces to march across Denmark. This is the army young Hamlet encounters in Act IV Scene 4, as he is about to embark for England. Young Hamlet is conscious of Young Fortinbras and what he stands for. His ambivalent reaction to encountering the Norwegian army is explored in the **Extended commentary** on **Text 3**.

This is also the army that marches back through Denmark, triumphant from Poland, at the end of the play. When Fortinbras visits Elsinore to pay Claudius his respects, he discovers that he has succeeded to the throne.

By the end of the play Young Fortinbras has more than realised his ambition. He has become King of Denmark. Ironically, he gives Hamlet a soldier's funeral.

THE PROBLEM OF THE GHOST

If there is a simple way of summing up Hamlet's moral dilemma in the play it is to be found in the Prince's response to his first sighting of the Ghost (I.4.38ff). Terrified, he wonders if this portentous figure, so like the father he eulogised in his first **soliloquy** (I.2.129ff), is 'a spirit of health or a goblin damned' (I.4.40), whether it brings with it pure air from heaven or contagion from hell, has intentions that are 'wicked or charitable'(I.4.42). The long moment of suspense generated by this threefold antithesis is used by Shakespeare to register in the audience's consciousness the idea of the ambiguous status of the Ghost.

Although it rejects Hamlet's pity, the Ghost's first move is to stir it up by describing his purgatorial suffering. In Act I Scene 5, lines 13–20, the Ghost terrifies Hamlet with the prospect of divine wrath but then calls upon Hamlet's sense of filial duty to commit a deed that will condemn him to it. The Ghost describes murder as 'most foul, as in the best it is' (I.5.27), and the murder of a king who is also a near relative as 'most foul, strange, and unnatural' (I.5.28) whilst asking the Prince to commit such a crime. It dwells luridly upon Gertrude's sexual depravity (I.5.53–7) but then tells Hamlet not to think ill of her.

Hamlet is being given a battery of double messages. They continue. Hamlet's mother is to be left to face God's judgement whilst Claudius is consigned to rough justice on earth. What authority has the Ghost to decide whom God should be left to punish? Is the Ghost 'the radiant angel' (I.5. 55) it paints itself as? The Ghost's moral code is a mass of contradictions.

During this encounter, Shakespeare signals to the audience Hamlet's unfitness for the role of **revenge hero** by the clever use of a confused simile. If we were asked to supply the missing words in this passage: 'Haste me to know't, that I with wings as swift / As .... / May sweep to my revenge' (I.5.29–31), we would probably offer something like 'thunderbolts or an avenging hawk'. Hamlet's lyrical words, 'meditation or the thoughts of love' are deliberately out of tune with the sentiments the situation demands. The Ghost's response is a cunning mixture of ironic praise

CHECK THE BOOK

'...the undying picture for me is that of great intellect hovering nearer and nearer to the brink – an intellect conscious of its own abstract grandeur, yet equally conscious of its concrete infirmity when faced with demand for action.' 'Irving as Hamlet' in *We Saw Him Act,* eds. H. A. Saintsbury and Cecil Palmer (1939).

and implied criticism: 'I find thee apt, / And duller shouldst thou be … / Wouldst thou not stir in this' (I.5.31–4). 'Dullness', and a feeling of failing to live up to what is expected of him, will be something Hamlet castigates himself for a number of times before sailing away from Denmark halfway through Act IV.

The Ghost's narrative of the murder (I.5.59ff) is graphic in its horrible details. The most interesting point about the story is that we never learn whether it is true. Why does Shakespeare invent such an elaborate and unusual method of killing someone, imprinting it on the audience's imagination by describing it in minutely disturbing detail?

Claudius confesses in Act III that he murdered his brother but he does not say *how* he murdered him. Despite having watched them represented twice on stage, he is haunted by none of the pictures of the disfigured corpse the Ghost paints. Perhaps Shakespeare is inviting us to explore the idea of somebody having poison poured into his ear metaphorically, and to ask whether this is what is happening in Act I Scene 5 to Hamlet.

It is these fascinating ambiguities in the Ghost's message that transform a play in the crude **revenge tragedy** tradition into sophisticated psychological drama. Hamlet is haunted by a figure closely resembling the man he thought of as a god. He spends the play vowing to obey instructions that he refuses to follow. Although he never articulates criticism of his father, Hamlet's actions speak louder than his words. Only when the Ghost is exorcised, in Act V, does the Prince claim the name he inherited from his father as his own.

QUESTION

How far, and in what ways, does the pursuit of revenge corrupt the avenger in the play *Hamlet*?

THEMES

REVENGE

The Elizabethan philosopher and statesman, Francis Bacon, condemned revenge as 'a kind of wild justice'. He argued 'it does… offend the law [and] putteth the law out of office'. The Christian Church insisted that vengeance was God's business not man's.

The ancient Roman religion of Fame prized family honour above all things. A man's reputation was all that lived after him; if he had been wronged, and the state failed to see that justice was done, a son's duty was to take the law into his own hands and seek revenge. Although revenge was a criminal offence in England, bloody, Roman-style revenge plays were very popular in London in the 1590s; Shakespeare's greatest hit in this genre was *Titus Andronicus*.

By the time Shakespeare came to rework the old play of *Hamlet,* revenge tragedies had developed certain conventional ingredients. Often there would be a Ghost, revealing how it had met its gruesome end through treachery. It would call upon the hero, for the sake of the family's honour, to settle accounts. Always there would be delay: what else could the play consist of? Delays due to plot and counter-plot in which sometimes the hero would pretend to be mad to catch his intended victim unawares. But, as if to endorse Bacon's condemnation of such 'wild justice', the price of revenge was conventionally the death of the person who carried it out. As the trailer for the 2003 film of *The Revenger's Tragedy* puts it, 'The man who seeks revenge should dig two graves.'

What Shakespeare does with these simple ingredients is to take them seriously. In the section on **The text**, we have shown how Young Fortinbras, Laertes and the Prince each respond to finding themselves cast as the hero in a revenge drama.

QUESTION

How far do you agree with the claim that in *Hamlet* the revenge plot deals out justice to all the characters?

In *Hamlet*, the incompatible value systems of the Roman and Christian codes of honour come into direct conflict to produce a far more complex revenge play than had ever been seen on the London stage. For Laertes and Fortinbras, there is no moral problem: both serve a simple code of honour which is rooted in family pride. Hamlet's case is far more complex. The Ghost talks like a Christian, telling his son there is judgement after death: he is suffering in purgatory. But what he demands of Hamlet sounds Roman and, if obeyed, would send his son to hell. Torn between duty to a Ghost who might be his father and obedience to his God, it is no wonder Hamlet delays his revenge, is puzzled by the identity of the Ghost and wrestles endlessly with his conscience.

MADNESS

> for to define true madness,
> What is't but to be nothing else but mad?   (II.2.93–4)

True to the conventions of revenge tragedy, Hamlet warns his friends that it is possible that he will pretend he is mad, will put on 'an antic disposition' (I.5.172) to help him carry out the Ghost's instructions. Whether Hamlet is ever mad, ever pretends to be mad or is considered mad by whom and at what times, is something over which critics of the play argue long and hard. No two performances will convey the same impression of the state of Hamlet's mind in the episodes that follow his interview with the Ghost in Act I Scene 5.

 QUESTION

'Hamlet does not play the madman; rather he plays the fool, mocking and telling truths that no one wants to hear.' Discuss.

Most, if not all, of the behaviour Ophelia describes in Act II Scene 1 sounds like play-acting. Hamlet appears to be doing what **revenge heroes** often do – trying to persuade his intended victim that he is a harmless madman so he will find it easier to carry out his task. But before he hears of this incident, Claudius tells us 'nor th'exterior nor the inward man' is like his former self (II.2.6–7). The person playing Hamlet, therefore, should probably be dressed oddly, not simply in black as he was in Act I Scene 2. And his behaviour must be more than bitterly melancholic as it was in that scene, if the audience is to understand the King's new anxiety.

We must remember that there is no such person in the world as Shakespeare's Hamlet; that he is a very cleverly made imitation of a real person but remains a human creation. Everything he does is the result of conscious or unconscious decisions made by Shakespeare.

We can see how Shakespeare presents 'pure' madness in Ophelia's behaviour in Act IV Scene 5. Her 'pretty' (line 41) nonsense can be presented as charming or disturbing but it is comprehensible and complete in itself: shock and bereavement make her 'incapable'. One of the dramatic purposes in presenting Ophelia's madness is to help the audience get a bearing upon Hamlet's.

The case would be much simpler if the Prince did not, in lines which are surely meant to sound sincere (V. 2.198–216), tell Laertes that he really has been mad. For most of the play when the Prince's madness has been a topic it has been clear to the audience that the term was a convenient fiction.

For example, often when Hamlet talks to Polonius, what sounds to the foolish old man like nonsense has a thread of bitter satire running through it. Hamlet's babble is not madness, but forthright contempt, privileged rudeness in a court where no one speaks the truth. Similarly, when Hamlet taunts Rosencrantz and Guildenstern he uses, as they realise, 'crafty madness' (III.1.8) to mock them and lead them astray. His behaviour is fully under his own control. Claudius asserts that his nephew is mad because he is convinced that he is not and he needs an excuse to get rid of the threat Hamlet poses. The Queen, in Act IV Scene 1, having watched Hamlet demonstrate his sanity, pretends her son is mad to excuse the murder of Polonius.

Hamlet's passionate exchanges with Ophelia and his mother may be violent – he himself talks of 'words like daggers' (III.4.95) – but what he says is both understandable and purposeful: he believes he is being 'cruel only to be kind' (III.4.179). If he punishes Ophelia harshly for her betrayal of him, we may not like it but we can understand it.

Madness can be defined as 'being in a minority of one'. Hamlet admires the one judicious person in the audience whose 'censure … must … o'erweigh a whole theatre of others' (III.2.20ff). If to be honest is to be 'one man picked out of ten thousand' (II.2.176), Hamlet is not afraid to be in a moral minority of one as his black clothes in Act I Scene 2 assert. Claudius tries to persuade Hamlet that his continued grieving for his father is 'to reason most absurd' (I.2.103) and since no one else in Elsinore is in mourning, we could believe that Claudius was right in suggesting Hamlet's 'obstinate condolement' (I.2.93) was evidence of 'a mind impatient' (I.2.96). However, in this case, we have Horatio's confirmation of how recent Hamlet's father's death was (Act I Scene 2) and some weeks later comes Gertrude's frank admission to her husband that Hamlet's 'distemper' (II.2.55) is most likely the result of 'His father's death, and [their] o'er hasty marriage' (II.2.57).

 READ THE BOOK

For a new-historicist essay examining madness in *Hamlet* in relation to Essex's dangerous subversion of Queen Elizabeth's authority in the 1590s, see Karin S. Coddon's 'Suche strange desygns, Madness, Subjectivity and Treason in *Hamlet* and Elizabethan Culture', reprinted in Susan Zimmerman (ed.), *New Casebooks, Shakespeare's Tragedies* (1998).

It is at moments of high excitement that Hamlet's behaviour is least comprehensible. His 'wild and whirling words' (I.5.133) following the Ghost's departure give way to the curious game he plays with 'this fellow in the cellarage' (I.5.150ff). In the confusion that ensues after the play-within-the-play (III.2.236ff), Hamlet is euphoric whilst Horatio is distinctly cool. It is in the major **soliloquies** that Hamlet's thinking is most confused. And, as we notice throughout the play, there is often a discrepancy between what Hamlet says he will do and his subsequent behaviour.

These interesting moments are the subject of detailed examination in the section on **The text**.

IMAGERY

The most distinctive feature of Shakespeare's poetry is the large number and great variety of images he uses. His characters express themselves graphically; there is very little abstract language.

**CHECK
THE BOOK**
The eighteenth-
century editor
Theobold was not
alone in finding the
mixed metaphor of
'Take arms against a
sea of troubles'
(III.1.59)
unsatisfactory.
Perhaps he made
the mistake of
blaming the poet
rather than the
Prince. Like the
confused metaphor
discussed above
(I.V.29–31), it
sharply conveys
Hamlet's sense of
being unequal to
the task confronting
him.

We are given strong mental pictures of the present and the particular. For example, instead of Horatio telling us it is daybreak, we get: 'But look, the morn in russet mantle clad / Walks o'er the dew of yon high eastward hill' (I.1.166–7). The Ghost's exit coincides with the entrance of a more powerful, lovelier figure. Polonius is ridiculed in caricature: 'That great baby you see there is not yet out of his swaddling clouts' (II.2.351). Hamlet describes his mother's adultery figuratively: 'Could you on this fair mountain leave to feed / And batten on this moor?' (III.4.66–7).

Personification, simile and metaphor make Shakespeare's language vivid, his ideas memorable. There are rich set pieces such as the Ghost's minutely detailed account of the effect of poison:

> … swift as quicksilver it courses through
> The natural gates and alleys of the body,
> And with a sudden vigour it doth posset
> And curd, like eager droppings into milk,
> The thin and wholesome blood …   (I.5.66–70)

We have the epic imagery of Hamlet's and the First Player's Trojan narratives (II.2.410ff) and Gertrude's pretty painting of Ophelia's drowning (IV.7.166ff). Usually, however, images are woven into what sounds like spontaneous dialogue: 'Happy in that we are not over-happy; on Fortune's cap we are not the very button' (II.2.220–21), or 'You must not think / That we are made of stuff so flat and dull / That we can let our beard be shook with danger / And think it pastime' (IV.7.30ff). Once the words are understood, they translate themselves into powerful imaginative experiences. And often images in one part of the play recall those heard earlier, as these words from Claudius echo, ironically, a passage in Hamlet's **soliloquy** (II.2.525ff).

This is true of Shakespeare's art generally. What gives *Hamlet* its particular tone is that many of the most powerful images in this tragedy are pictures of disease and corruption. In the first moments of the play we hear that Francisco is 'sick at heart' (I.1.9). Marcellus speaking like a **Chorus** is certain: 'Something is rotten in the state of Denmark' (I.4.90). Hamlet feels the country is like 'an unweeded garden' populated entirely by 'things rank and gross in nature' (I.2.135–6). And as the play develops, we are made to feel that Elsinore is an unhealthy place. Her brother warns Ophelia of the risk of 'contagious blastments' (I.3.42); Hamlet reminds Polonius that even the sun 'breed[s] maggots in a dead dog' and that he must keep his daughter safe (II.2.179ff). At Ophelia's funeral, Laertes asserts his sister's innocence like this: 'And from her fair and unpolluted flesh / May violets spring.' (V.1.206–7), a dramatic contrast with what the Gravedigger has just told us. He deals with 'many pocky corses nowadays that will scarce hold the laying in' (V.1.140). Hamlet reflects on degeneration of the kingdom where 'the toe of the peasant comes so near the heel of the courtier, he galls his kibe' (V.1.117).

What is the origin of these sores, this sickness and corruption? At the heart of the 'unweeded garden' is a throne polluted by regicide, fratricide, adultery and incest. To cleanse it is Hamlet's overwhelming task. Planning *The Mousetrap*, he imagines himself to be a surgeon who will 'tent [Claudius] to the quick' (II.2.550). In being 'cruel only to be kind' (III.4.179) to his mother, he describes

CHECK THE NET

An online *Hamlet* concordance (useful for exploring imagery) will be found at: **http:// www. concordance.com**.

QUESTION

'Something is rotten in the state of Denmark'. In what ways does Shakespeare suggest a general sense of corruption in *Hamlet*?

her sin as if it were physical disease which must not be neglected: 'It will but skin and film the ulcerous place, / Whiles rank corruption, mining all within, / Infects unseen' (II.2.148–50). He uses a similar image to describe the decadent behaviour of Fortinbras's army, where twenty thousand men will lose their lives for nothing: 'This is the imposthume ... / That inward breaks, and shows no cause without / Why the man dies' (IV.4.27–29).

It is not only Hamlet whose 'wit's diseased' (III.2.291). Claudius, staggering under the 'heavy burden' (III.1.54) of his sins, feels that Hamlet is his plague: 'like the hectic in my blood he rages' (IV.3.62). As early as Act II Scene 2, he is thinking of a possible 'remedy' (II.2.18). And by the time he ships him off to England he tells us: 'Diseases desperate grown / By desperate appliance are relieved, / Or not at all' (IV.3.9–11).

Hamlet escapes one snare. Claudius, plotting Hamlet's murder a second time, uses Hamlet's own image from Act II Scene 2 to emphasise to Laertes the need for drastic surgery: 'But, to the quick of th'ulcer' (IV.7.122).

Diseased bodies become pocky corpses. Towards the end of the play, the imagery of corruption takes on a darker hue:

> CLAUDIUS: Now Hamlet, where's Polonius? ...
> HAMLET: Not where he eats, but where a is eaten. A certain convocation of politic worms are e'en at him. ... Your fat king and your lean beggar is but ... two dishes, but to one table ... a king may go a progress through the guts of a beggar.
>
> (IV. 3.16ff)

Disease, madness, corruption and decay. Horatio fears Ophelia's distraction may 'strew / Dangerous conjectures in ill-breeding minds' (IV.5.14–15). Later we hear the people of Denmark are indeed 'Thick and unwholesome in their thoughts and whispers' (IV.5.81).

Images of prostitution run through the play as a complement to the imagery of disease. In Hamlet's eyes both the women in his life fall

CHECK THE FILM
One of the most successful of the Animated Tales was Natalia Orlova's 1992 version of *Hamlet*. For an analysis of the film see 'Poetry in Motion' by Laurie E. Osborne in (eds.) Lynda E. Boose and Richard Burt, *Shakespeare the Movie* (1997).

short of the ideal he presents in *The Mousetrap*. In a particularly disturbing picture, Hamlet sees Gertrude's sexual misconduct as the source of the moral pollution that has tarnished his relationship with Ophelia: 'an act / That blurs the grace and blush of modesty, / … takes off the rose / From the fair forehead of an innocent love / And sets a blister there' (III.4.40–44). The violent juxtaposition of images: the beautiful, fragrant, fragile rose, symbolic of youth and innocence, set alongside the blistered forehead of a branded prostitute is shocking. Interestingly, Claudius compares himself to a whore being whipped through the streets:

> How smart a lash that speech doth give my conscience!
> The harlot's cheek, beautied with plastering art,
> Is not more ugly to the thing that helps it
> Than is my deed to my most painted word.
>
> (III.1.50–3)

By Act V Scene 2, Hamlet is convinced of his moral responsibility to kill the criminal King who, 'like a mildewed ear / [Blasted] his wholesome brother' (III.4.64–5) and is infecting the whole country: 'is't not to be damned / To let this canker of our nature come / Into further evil?' (V.2.68–70).

CHECK THE BOOK

For a study of the prevalence of the theme of prostitution in *Hamlet*, see 'Hamlet's Whores' by Kay Stanton in *New Essays on Hamlet*, eds. Mark Thornton Burnett and John Manning (1994).

PART FOUR

CRITICAL HISTORY

 CHECK THE BOOK

Victor Hugo contrasts Hamlet with Aeschylus' character Prometheus: 'Prometheus is action. Hamlet is hesitation. In Prometheus, the obstacle is exterior; in Hamlet it is interior. In Prometheus, the will is securely nailed down by nails of brass and cannot get loose ... In Hamlet the will is more tied down yet, it is bound by previous meditation, the endless chain of the undecided ... Prometheus, in order to be free, has but a bronze collar to break and a god to conquer; Hamlet must break and conquer himself', *William Shakespeare* (1864).

When the **First Folio** of Shakespeare's works appeared in 1623, it was published so that people could 'reade him ... againe and againe'. From the appearance of the pirated **Quarto** of 1603 and the authorised one of 1604, it was evident that *Hamlet* was already popular not only as a stage play but also as a text to be read, savoured and, no doubt, hotly debated.

Over the last four hundred years, *Hamlet* has become the most frequently performed play of all time. And its popularity is global. It has been translated into dozens of languages and there have been over eighty cinema and television films made of the play and about the play. These films have reached a worldwide audience. With this popularity has come intense critical activity. No literary text in history has been the subject of so much human interrogation as Shakespeare's *Hamlet*. An Internet search engine will reveal some seventy thousand web sites devoted to *Hamlet* topics.

Because there has been so much written about *Hamlet* the play, about Hamlet the character and about *Hamlet* criticism itself, what follows can be no more than the crudest outline of some of the ways critics of different generations have responded to the many interesting problems Shakespeare has left us with. The section **Further reading** contains numerous suggestions.

SEVENTEENTH-CENTURY CRITICISM

The earliest surviving allusion to a play called *Hamlet* is made by Thomas Nashe in 1589; Henslowe records a production in 1594; and in 1596, Thomas Lodge recalls a play with a character looking 'as pale as the Visard of the Ghost which cried so miserably at the theatre, like an oister wife, "Hamlet, revenge." ' Since we believe that Shakespeare's *Hamlet* dates from about 1601, these tantalising references suggest that an earlier play of *Hamlet*, which most scholars think was probably written by Thomas Kyd, was already familiar to London audiences in the 1590s. It may be that Shakespeare revised the old play.

Although there is little of what we would call formal criticism of
Shakespeare's play before the eighteenth century, the evidence of eye-
witnesses suggest that *Hamlet* was an immediate popular success.
Samuel Pepys and John Evelyn, the famous diarists, both record
attending performances. What is curious about early comments on
this most thought-provoking of plays, however, is that few of the
'problems' which have exercised critics for the last three hundred
years seem to have bothered Shakespeare's near-contemporaries.

 **CHECK
THE BOOK**
A rich source of
early critical
reactions to *Hamlet*
is David Farley-Hill's
three-volume work,
*Critical Responses to
Hamlet 1600–1854*
(1996–9).

EIGHTEENTH-CENTURY CRITICISM

It was Thomas Hanmer in 1736 who drew attention to Hamlet's
delay in carrying out his revenge. Delay was one of the conventions
of **revenge tragedy** that Shakespeare inherited, and Hanmer makes
the practical point that had the Prince carried out his father's
instructions straight away 'there would have been an End of our
Play'. But this has not prevented later critics seeing the delay of
which Hamlet accuses himself before the Ghost returns to 'whet
[his] almost blunted purpose' (III.4.110) as a matter requiring
investigation along psychological lines.

In 1762, Tobias Smollett examined Hamlet's most celebrated
soliloquy (III.1.56–88) and found in its confused metaphors 'a heap
of absurdities, whether we consider the situation, the sentiment, the
argumentation or the poetry'; Dr Johnson, perceiving that the
confusion arose from 'a man distracted with contrariety of desires
and overwhelmed with the magnitude of his own purposes' sought
to demonstrate how the thought of the soliloquy 'is connected
rather in the speaker's mind, than on his tongue.'

Meanwhile the French philosopher Voltaire, judging the playwright
by the prescriptions of neo-classical critical theory, declared in 1733,
'Shakespeare boasted a strong fruitful Genius: He was natural and
sublime, but had not so much as a single Spark of good Taste, or
knew one Rule of the Drama ... the great Merit of this Dramatic
Poet has been the Ruin of the English Stage.' He was particularly
scathing about *Hamlet*, writing in 1748, 'one would think that this
work was the fruit of the imagination of a drunken savage.'

ROMANTICISM

Towards the end of the eighteenth century and during the Romantic period, Shakespeare himself was elevated almost to the status of a God; suggestions that anything he produced was less than transcendental came to be regarded as blasphemy. Hamlet became a figure exciting intense speculation, partly because the spiritual agony and searing insight of an individual alienated from society was a theme so close to the Romantic sensibility. Hamlet invited identification; the complexity of his thoughts and the ambiguity of his actions made him appear 'life-like' because he could not easily be summed up. And since there is throughout the play a preoccupation with madness, another favourite theme in Romantic literature, Hamlet began to be talked about as if he were someone in real life, existing at times independently of the rest of the play. The great German poet Goethe, for example, claimed to feel a kinship with this sixteenth-century Anglo-Danish prince.

As people began to scrutinise the text ever more closely, there developed a strong feeling that, like the greatest music, *Hamlet* was better enjoyed in the privacy of the study than in some clumsy performance. Of *Hamlet,* William Hazlitt writing in 1817 said, 'There is no play that suffers so much in being transferred to the stage'.

CHECK THE NET

Coleridge's 1818 lecture on *Hamlet* will be found at: **http:// shakespearean. org.uk/ham1-col. htm**.

The Romantic poet and critic Samuel Coleridge saw in the Prince a man whose intellectual energy and alertness understandably made action impossible. Like Goethe and many lesser critics, he sensed 'a smack of Hamlet' in himself. In an age which felt that progress and alienation were natural bedfellows, Hamlet became in William Hazlitt's words 'the most amiable of misanthropes'.

EARLY TWENTIETH-CENTURY CRITICISM

Throughout the nineteenth century and for much of the twentieth, criticism of *Hamlet* took the form of character analysis: largely of the Prince himself but also of Claudius, Gertrude and Ophelia. In Hamlet's case, delay having been diagnosed as his besetting shortcoming, the critic's task was to account for it, if not excuse and eulogise it. The assumption was that the hero had a character that was stable, fathomable and largely distinct from any social function. For Goethe, the case was thus: 'A lovely, pure, noble and most moral nature … sinks beneath a burden which it cannot bear and must not cast away'. But perhaps there were practical obstacles. Was Claudius so shrewd and well protected that Hamlet could not, even if he wished to, have found him alone before Act III Scene 4? Or was there an instinctive but inexpressible moral repugnance with the Ghost's 'commandment' (I.5.102) that the tortured **soliloquies** attempted unsuccessfully to rationalise? Perhaps Hamlet's wit really was 'diseased' (III.2.300), enervated by the foul moral climate in which his sensitive soul had its being.

One of the most eloquent and influential essays written on *Hamlet* appeared in 1904. As one of a series of lectures on Shakespearean Tragedy, A. C. Bradley's exploration of Hamlet as a son made melancholy by his mother's sexual depravity, who can respond to the Ghost's demand for action in words but not in deed, explored territory that has been frequently revisited. A. C. Bradley tends to treat *Hamlet* as if it were a nineteenth-century novel rather than a sixteenth-century play. But his careful attention to, and delight in, textual detail made an important contribution to the progress of Shakespearean studies and remains one of the handful of essays on the play which every student should explore. However, Bradley falls into the trap of trying to reduce all Shakespearean tragedy to a formula: the tragic hero is someone suffering from a particular weakness of character. If Macbeth's 'tragic flaw' is ambition and Othello's is jealousy, then what must Hamlet's be? It is a temptation towards simplification to which all generalising theories are prone.

Ernest Jones's essay on *Hamlet* appeared in 1949. It takes the psychoanalysis of the characters in the play as if they were people in real life to a conveniently extreme position, suggesting that Hamlet's problem is that he has an Oedipus complex. How can he murder Claudius when his uncle has committed the deed he himself subconsciously wished to carry out? Fascinated by what disgusts him, Hamlet is understandably paralysed. As John Jump shrewdly observes: 'Students … are likely to feel that [Ernest Jones's] Hamlet owes more to Freud's imagination than to Shakespeare's'.

CHECK THE BOOK

For a critical examination of psychoanalytic approaches to Shakespeare in general and to *Hamlet* in particular, see *Shakespeare in Psychoanalysis* by Philip Armstrong (2001).

By the time T. S. Eliot's essay on *Hamlet* was published (1919), the play was acquiring the distinction of being endlessly 'problematic'.

On the whole, critics relished rather than regretted this. In a characteristically obtuse approach, T. S. Eliot proclaimed that the problem was the play itself. It was an artistic failure. Shakespeare, he maintained, was struggling to articulate a disgust he could not account for. Gertrude and her misdemeanours were out of all proportion to the anguish we were shown they caused her son. If we remember that the essay was written just before *The Waste Land*, we can see that, like so many essays on this play, T. S. Eliot's is as useful for what it tells us about the critic's own development as an artist as for what light it sheds upon Shakespeare's. But its robustness let in some much-needed fresh air. The very suggestion that not everything Shakespeare produced was immaculate might have been regarded as a heresy in the preceding century. T. S. Eliot's scepticism was an advance on bardology.

But what weaned criticism of *Hamlet* away from the kind of subjective and exclusive exploration of character into which it was in danger of stagnating, was the work of two very different critics, Harley Granville-Barker and John Dover Wilson.

Harley Granville-Barker, like Shakespeare himself, was a practical man of the theatre. By encouraging students to examine *Hamlet* once again as a play in performance, his *Preface to Hamlet*, which came out in 1936, signalled a refreshing change of focus.

John Dover Wilson's contribution to the *Hamlet* debate was even more fundamental and far-reaching in its consequences. In his Cambridge edition of the play, which first appeared in 1934, he challenged the authority of the **First Folio** as the source upon which editors should base their texts. He drew attention to qualities in the **Second Quarto** and to a number of details absent from or strikingly different in the Folio text. If his advocacy of the Second Quarto as the 'authentic' text of Shakespeare's play has since been overtaken by the research which has now given us not one but two or even three 'authentic' *Hamlet* texts, his painstaking attention to detail and his awareness of how such details must influence performance was

**CHECK
THE BOOK**

'If Shakespeare were stript of all the Bombast in his passions, and dress'd in the most vulgar words, we should find the beauties of his thoughts remaining; if his embroideries were burnt down, there would still be silver at the bottom of the melting-pot: but I fear...that we who Ape his sounding words, have nothing of his thought, but are all out-side; there is not so much as a dwarf within our Giant's cloaths.'
John Dryden,
Preface to Troilus and Cressida (1679).

instrumental in compelling students to base their critical speculations much more firmly on close textual scrutiny and extended commentary. And although Dover Wilson's subsequent volume on the play, *What Happens in Hamlet*, has a title that suggests to the unwary that here at last is a definitive reading, his reminders about Elizabethan theatrical practice and Elizabethan mores are usefully provocative. Dover Wilson more clearly than any critic before him articulated the ambiguous nature of the Ghost and the impossibility of Hamlet's translating its instructions into a coherent plan of action.

With Caroline Spurgeon and G. Wilson Knight, a new approach to Shakespearean criticism emerged. Rather than separating individuals for psychological investigation, what both critics explored was the role of imagery in the plays. Metaphors and similes are the lifeblood of poetry. Something that becomes apparent to anyone who reads and reads again their Shakespeare, as the publishers of the **First Folio** hoped they would, is that Shakespeare's images often form clusters. In certain plays, there are large numbers of particular kinds of images. What Caroline Spurgeon identified in *Hamlet* was 'the number of images of sickness, disease ... the idea of an ulcer or tumour, as descriptive of the unwholesome condition of Denmark morally'. It is in this climate of pestilence that Hamlet inevitably succumbs. G. Wilson Knight saw Shakespeare's plays less as drama than as poems whose highly wrought language generates their distinctive ambience and meaning. For Wilson Knight, the Prince is not a heroic victim but a sinister presence in Denmark. In his aptly titled study, *Hamlet The Prince or the Poem?*, C. S. Lewis describes *Hamlet* less as the history of a particular individual than as a picture of alienated mankind struggling to discover meaning. Like G. Wilson Knight, L. C. Knights presented a reading of *Hamlet* that challenged Romantic notions of the hero. L. C. Knights sees the Prince's judgements as brooding upon evil, pathologically unbalanced.

 **CHECK THE BOOK**

In *The Wheel of Fire* (1930), G. Wilson Knight describes Hamlet as 'an inhuman – or superhuman – presence, whose consciousness – somewhat like Dostoyevsky's Stavrogin – is centred on death. Like Stavrogin, he is feared by those around him. They are always trying to find out what is wrong with him. They cannot understand him. He is a creature of another world'.

RECENT DEVELOPMENTS IN *HAMLET* CRITICISM

Over the last thirty years, new and radical critical theories have emerged. They ask us to reconsider the way people read any literary text, *Hamlet* included. This does not mean that the ways A. C.

CHECK THE BOOK

For an overview of recent approaches to *Hamlet*, see Michael Hattaway's *Hamlet: The Critics Debate* (1987).

CHECK THE BOOK

In *Critical Essays on Shakespeare's Hamlet* (1995), George T. Wright notes that in *Hamlet* 'Shakespeare uses **hendiadys** both to explore his characters and to probe his themes...In the great enigma of *Hamlet*, this perplexing figure serves to remind us, in comic and tragic moments, how uncertain and treacherous language and behavior can be.'

Bradley, for example, John Dover Wilson or G. Wilson Knight examined *Hamlet* are no longer valid or that students must ditch lines of enquiry that have proved so fruitful in the past. But awareness of very different ways of thinking about texts is not only prudent but stimulating. Like any radical departure, recent critical theory will in time become integrated with the approaches of earlier generations, helping us to see more clearly what any single type of critical analysis can and cannot achieve.

Traditional theories see *Hamlet* as a work of art that must be taken as it stands, much of the critic's job being to show how apparently discordant elements within the play relate to one another in a meaningful and persuasive way which engages with perennial human concerns. We are encouraged to study *Hamlet* as a coherent work which, in the Prince's own phrase, 'holds the mirror up to nature' (III.2.18–19), and to examine what Shakespeare is showing us in this drama about human life and human responsibilities.

There is still much mileage in such investigations. In his introduction to the New Cambridge edition (1985), Philip Edwards explores vigorously once again the ethical dilemmas posed by the clash of two incompatible moral codes, relating this drama to the fractious religious context in which Shakespeare produced his work.

What distinguishes radical late-twentieth-century and twenty-first century thinkers about the play from those of earlier generations is above all their rejection of the idea that any work or any author can achieve the kind of universality and stability that generations of critics have claimed for *Hamlet* in particular and for Shakespeare more generally – the idea crystallised by Ben Jonson in his tribute to Shakespeare that 'He was not of an age, but for all time'. Catherine Belsey talks of 'the myth of an unchanging human nature'. What such critics stress is the way that any work of art mirrors the beliefs, assumptions, prejudices and blind spots of the society in which it is produced. That no individual can be said to transcend the circumstances in which s/he operates and that any reading is similarly, decisively shaped by the intellectual climate in which it takes place. A play may not so much reflect social reality as be a reflection on social reality. Recent criticism also points to the simple fact that the language itself is volatile: what we take Shakespeare's words to mean and what they may have meant four hundred years ago is at the very least something demanding critical attention.

STRUCTURALISM & POST-STRUCTURALISM

Structuralist critics approach *Hamlet* as they would any other statement, as an interesting linguistic phenomenon. Rather than search the play in the hope of finding that it tells something about the world or human nature or the relationship of humanity to eternity, structuralists explore the ways in which key words generate about them force fields of associations and value systems and thus mean more than is immediately apparent. Or mean something rather different from what they may appear to mean to the untrained observer.

In *New Essays on Hamlet*, first published in 1994, the editor, Mark Thornton Burnett, talks of the unlimited range of meanings to be found in *Hamlet* and concludes that:

> Abundantly evident ... is *Hamlet*'s refusal to fit into neat categorizations, its resistance to generic classifications and its unwillingness to affirm cherished ideals.

He shows that *Hamlet* revels in asking questions about identity and that, indeed, the posing and answering of questions is one of the play's most striking features. *Hamlet*'s delight in doubling characters and situations contributes to the play's subversion of any straightforward reading, and helps 'to deny the closure that is only ever promised but never delivered'.

Taking this scepticism a stage further, post-structuralists insist upon the ambiguity of any statement or work of art. This differs radically from the belief of critics such as William Empson, that, on the whole, great poets use ambiguity deliberately and in a controlled manner to achieve particular results. Post-structuralism argues that a work of art has no primary or final meaning and that engaging with *Hamlet*, like engaging with anything else, is like a perpetual series of chess games in which there will be an almost infinite number of outcomes, none of which is superior to any other, simply

CHECK THE BOOK

A product of American new-historicist criticism is Stephan Greenblatt's *Hamlet in Purgatory* (2001), which attempts to 'understand what Shakespeare inherited and transformed' from medieval and contemporary sixteenth-century debates about the nature of purgatory in his dramatisation of the theme in *Hamlet*: 'I believe nothing comes from nothing, even in Shakespeare. I wanted to know where he got the matter he was working with and what he did with that matter'.

different. Post-structuralist criticism revels in the intricate ways language works to generate a rich and bewildering complex of possible meanings.

Other critical approaches which inform a great deal of contemporary thinking about *Hamlet* are less concerned with linguistic studies in a vacuum than with the need to address the political agenda with which it is argued any work of literature consciously or unconsciously presents us.

FEMINIST CRITICISM

Feminist criticism, like any other school of criticism, speaks with many different voices. Common to all feminists, however, is the desire to challenge and change assumptions about gender, illuminating the way in which sexual stereotyping and assumptions about sexual roles are frequently embodied in a text, in the ways critics have responded to a text and in the ways texts have been re-presented on the stage, in films and in other media. Literature and the ways in which it has been written about in the past are seen as having contributed to the marginalisation of women and to denying women a voice.

 QUESTION

'Frailty, thy name is woman!' In what ways does this comment help to illuminate the play *Hamlet*?

It has been noted in the section on **The text** that in *Hamlet* neither Gertrude nor Ophelia is developed as fully as Hamlet or Claudius; quite simply Shakespeare gives them far less stage time and far fewer lines than Hamlet's concern with them might lead us to expect. Rather than see this as a compromise dictated by pragmatic theatrical considerations, feminist criticism looks at the 'silencing' of the women as an important part of the play's meaning. A consequence of this 'silencing', however, leads feminist critics to examine the ways different productions of *Hamlet*, on stage and screen, use non-verbal language to make statements about the place of women in the world of the play. Such criticism reminds us forcibly that what we have in *Hamlet* is something not just to be read but also to be acted, and that in performance the words may provide only part of what any audience is asked to respond to.

Feminist criticism has also explored the ways in which readers, audiences and other artists have responded to Shakespeare's

Gertrude and Ophelia, the latter having achieved a degree of autonomy from Shakespeare's play and become, particularly through paintings, an icon of woman as victim. This leads into the interesting territory of how different societies have incorporated aspects or partial readings of *Hamlet* into wider use so that, in advertising for example, some of Shakespeare's words or the graveyard **tableau** have developed an existence independent of the play.

But critics interested in gender issues have not confined their attention to Shakespeare's presentation of women in *Hamlet*. If, as in *Macbeth*, one of the hero's problems is trying to answer the question, 'What is a man…?' (IV.4.33ff.), a number of contemporary studies have returned to the examination of Hamlet's perplexity about what constitutes appropriate behaviour for human beings as distinct from beasts, men as distinct from women. In this area, psychological, moral and sociological kinds of enquiry combine to sustain the fascination that studying this play has exerted over the centuries.

POLITICAL CRITICISM

> It is not the consciousness of men that determines their being but on the contrary, their social being that determines their consciousness.
>
>   Marx, *Preface to the Critique of Political Economy*

A different kind of political scrutiny of the play has developed in the form of Marxist criticism and the 'new historicism', of which the new Norton Shakespeare, edited by Stephen Greenblatt and others, may be regarded as something of a flagship. As in feminist so in Marxist criticism, it is contended that there can be no reading of *Hamlet* that is not 'political'. Critics such as Catherine Belsey probe the conflicting notions of authority and power that give rise to so much of the dramatic interest in the play. One interesting shift has been the prominence now accorded to the part played by Fortinbras in the drama. It was quite common in nineteenth century productions to cut the Fortinbras strand entirely. Some modern critics argue that it is on the character of Fortinbras that the 'politics' of *Hamlet* hinge; Branagh's film gives the Norwegian's prince's exploits unusual prominence.

CHECK THE BOOK

For a feminist reading of Ophelia and the way male criticism has treated her, see Elaine Showalter's essay *Representing Ophelia: Women, Madness and the Responsibilities of Feminist Criticism* in Martin Coyle (ed.) *New Casebooks: Hamlet* (1992).

QUESTION

'The production which does not set the personal tragedy in a firm context of state affairs misses much of the play.' Discuss this view of *Hamlet*.

But whereas earlier critics determine to find ways to resolve apparent contradictions and inconsistencies, whether within a single speech or in the larger design of the play, Marxist approaches more commonly offer the revelation of fallibility masked by the illusion of coherence to which not only Shakespeare but also those who have written upon him subsequently have contributed.

What is consistently challenged is the idea that there can be a 'common-sense' response to any text. If authors are influenced by their historical and cultural circumstances, so too are audiences and readers. *Hamlet* was produced at a time of unprecedented intellectual ferment; religious and political controversy in a London which at the turn of the seventeenth century pointed towards the civil war and its resulting new conceptions of authority within fifty years.

CHECK THE BOOK

For a political reading of Hamlet, see Jan Kott's book *Shakespeare Our Contemporary* (1964).

The new historicists call attention to the fact that this play, which dramatises upheavals in the royal court, was written at a time when the absolute power of the monarchy was being tested by the irresistible rise of capitalism. Hamlet is at once a king's son, Claudius's heir and a voice that expresses disgust with those in power. The new historicists, unlike the practitioners of the 'new criticism', are concerned less with the words on the page than with the circumstances in which they were produced. Ideology, the whole value system which informs any utterance, and the reception of any utterance shifts the critical focus from the particular author and the particular work of art to the complex value systems in which it came into being. Rather than *Hamlet* being a powerful creative expression of Shakespeare's understanding of the universal and timeless human condition, the play is seen as a product of Elizabethan culture as it passed through a period of extraordinary upheaval. *Hamlet* dramatises the struggles of its time. Such approaches, drawing as they often do upon generalisations not only about Shakespeare's art as a whole but also about Renaissance thought and the processes of early modern culture, stand in marked contrast to the meticulous preoccupation with each particular image, word and gesture, which characterised a great deal of *Hamlet* criticism in the first half of the present century.

Yet labels can be misleading. In its scrupulously text-centred argument, there is little in Victor Kiernan's searching examination of *Hamlet*, in *Eight Tragedies of Shakespeare, A Marxist Study* (1996), which distinguishes it from the character analyst's approach. In taking account of the political dimensions of Hamlet's situation, he does not elevate them in importance above that of Hamlet's active consciousness which he identifies closely with Shakespeare's own: 'Hamlet himself can be thought of as probably like many Elizabethans, a mixture of Christian and pagan and sceptic'.

ORIGINAL TEXTS

Perhaps the most radical challenge to long-received notions of *Hamlet* and its problems for all of us has come about as a result of the research that culminated in the new Oxford Edition of the works of Shakespeare edited by Stanley Wells and Gary Taylor (1988). Ever since the eighteenth century, the texts that readers and audiences have known as *Hamlet* have been texts which Shakespeare's company would not have recognised. Until very recently, editors have agreed to use the three earliest versions of the play which have come down to us as sources from which they could 'mix and match', taking what they thought to be the best of each and synthesising a version of the play they believed Shakespeare to have written. As with *King Lear*, so with *Hamlet,* the Oxford editors have argued: we are likely to find ourselves closer to understanding Shakespeare's work if we recognise that in the light of his experience with the play on stage, Shakespeare revised his work, and that the text we find in the **First Folio** is a different *Hamlet* from the one first seen by London audiences. This means that many of the editions of the play currently studied in schools and universities have at best a qualified claim to authenticity. The Alexander text, with which until recently most editions were more or less in line, has been a cultural artefact that has entertained audiences and readers and exercised critical minds for many years. We are living in a new era. To add to all the other reasons why *Hamlet* continues to fascinate, provoke and frustrate those who would like to offer a definitive interpretation of the play, we have now the existence of several different texts of *Hamlet*, each with claims to be taken seriously.

 CHECK THE BOOK

'Yet even though the memorial reconstruction hypothesis accounts for a number of Q1's special features, especially its flaws, it does not explain the many other features that seem to be the result of skilful theatrical adaptation.' Kathleen O. Irace (ed.), *The First Quarto of Hamlet* (1998).

READ THE BOOK

Stanley Wells's *Shakespeare in the Theatre, An Anthology of Criticism* (1997), includes vivid first-hand accounts of many performances, from the eighteenth to the late twentieth century.

CHECK THE FILM

'As a text that supports the dominant fiction of the Oedipal fantasy, Branagh's *Hamlet* is a "squeaky clean" adaptation...one that reinforces conservative ideology and cultural values...the most Oedipal of all *Hamlets* on screen, despite its director's denials.' Lisa S. Starks, 'The displaced body of desire: Sexuality in Kenneth Branagh's *Hamlet*' in *Shakespeare and Appropriation* (1999).

PERFORMANCE CRITICISM

...the text of the play is only its starting point...only in production is its potential realized and capable of being appreciated fully. Shakespeare is only one collaborator in the creation and infinite recreation of his play...

J. S. Bratton and Julie Hankey,
series editors, *Shakespeare in Production*

Deconstruction, feminism, 'history of ideas' criticism, Freudian and Jungian analyses, new historicism, Marxism, genre theory, philosophical approaches, bibliography, myth criticism...

Faced with the Byzantine speculations of much recent criticism, the student for whom *Hamlet* is still a fresh and lively area of experience may find the newly-respectable area of criticism known as 'performance criticism' not only the most approachable but also the most rewarding.

Hamlet has been performed more than any other play in the history of literature. Some of the most penetrating twentieth-century criticism of Shakespeare's play is to be found not in critical essays but in the increasingly large stock of performances of the play now available to students on DVD and the Internet. Many of the dozens of film versions, some silent ones dating back to the beginning of the twentieth century, are now becoming available for students to compare with spectacular contemporary productions.

Every performance is an interpretation. It is not simply a matter of casting, acting styles, tones of voice, costume, sets, and all the 'business' that directors interpolate. Most productions cut the text even more severely than Shakespeare appears to have done himself. Where those cuts are made throws what is left into a new relief. To watch a single scene, such as *The Mousetrap* episode, in productions as strikingly dissimilar from one another as Laurence Olivier's, Kozinstev's, Coronado's, Rodney Bennet's, Tony Richardson's and Kenneth Brannagh's, for example, is to realise with a fresh immediacy the potential this play, perhaps more than any other, has for radically different, challenging readings.

For the most part, actors and directors approach Shakespeare's text from a pragmatic rather than from a theoretical or dogmatic standpoint, informed by four centuries of practical experience of what makes *Hamlet* work with audiences. There is far more sense of continuity between one generation of actors and the next than between successive generations of critics. When productions have tried too single-mindedly to apply an apparently plausible but eccentric critical reading the result has usually been a very short run.

A thought-provoking study of how Shakespeare's *Hamlet* was first presented in the Elizabethan playhouses is provided in Andrew Gurr and Mariko Ichikawa's *Staging in Shakespeare's Theatres* (2000). Robert Hapgood's *Shakespeare in Production: Hamlet* (1999), contains a fine overview of *Hamlet* on stage and film from Burbage to Branagh. It also gives the complete New Cambridge text of the play with detailed annotations recording eye-witness accounts, contemporary criticism, prompt-book marginalia, cuts, additions and rewritings showing various ways in which performance practices over the last four hundred years have shaped the re-presentation of particular episodes and speeches. Two experienced men of the theatre have also provided invaluable commentaries on the staging of *Hamlet*: Harley Granville Barker's *Prefaces to Shakespeare, Hamlet* (1936) raised questions and made observations of a kind which would occur naturally to a practising actor but might not to an armchair critic. *Hamlet, A User's Guide* by Michael Pennington (1996) is an insider's, scene-by-scene 'sawdust scholarship' account of many modern productions.

This is a rich and growing field of study. Several other books analysing the presentation of Shakespeare in the theatre, on film and on television are listed under **Further reading**.

CHECK THE BOOK

Robert Shaughnessy's collection of essays, *Shakespeare in Performance* (2000), examines the debates between theory and practice that have transformed our understanding of Shakespeare performance in recent years. Drawing upon textual theory, materialist cultural criticism, new historicism, feminism, post-colonialism, and psychoanalysis, the essays address Shakespeare's plays as texts in and for performance in a variety of contexts, from the Renaissance to the present.

PART FIVE

BACKGROUND

WILLIAM SHAKESPEARE'S LIFE

There are no personal records of Shakespeare's life. Official documents and occasional references to him by contemporary dramatists enable us to draw the main outline of his public life, but his private life remains hidden. Although not at all unusual for a writer of his time, this lack of first-hand evidence has tempted many to read his plays as personal records and to look in them for clues to Shakespeare's character and convictions. The results are unconvincing, partly because Renaissance art was not subjective or designed primarily to express its creator's personality, and partly because the drama of any period is very difficult to read biographically. Except when plays are written by committed dramatists to promote social or political causes (as by Shaw or Brecht), it is all but impossible to decide who amongst the variety of fictional characters in a drama represents the dramatist, or which of the various and often conflicting points of view expressed is authorial.

What we do know can be quickly summarised. Shakespeare was born into a well-to-do family in the market town of Stratford-upon-Avon in Warwickshire, where he was baptised, in Holy Trinity Church, on 26 April 1564. His father, John Shakespeare, was a prosperous glover and leather merchant who became a person of some importance in the town: in 1565 he was elected an alderman of the town, and in 1568 he became high bailiff (or mayor) of Stratford. In 1557 he had married Mary Arden. Their third child (of eight) and eldest son, William, learned to read and write at the primary (or 'petty') school in Stratford and then, it seems probable, attended the local grammar school, where he would have studied Latin, history, logic and rhetoric. In November 1582 William, then aged eighteen, married Anne Hathaway, who was twenty-six years old. They had a daughter, Susanna, in May 1583, and twins, Hamnet and Judith, in 1585.

CHECK THE BOOK

There are a number of biographies of Shakespeare – many of them very speculative – but the most authoritative is still Samuel Schoenbaum's *Shakespeare: A Documentary Life* (1975).

Shakespeare next appears in the historical record in 1592 when he is mentioned as a London actor and playwright in a pamphlet by the dramatist Robert Greene. These 'lost years' 1585–92 have been the subject of much speculation, but how they were occupied remains as much a mystery as when Shakespeare left Stratford, and why. In his pamphlet, *Greene's Groatsworth of Wit*, Greene expresses to his fellow dramatists his outrage that the 'upstart crow' Shakespeare has the impudence to believe he 'is as well able to bombast out a blank verse as the best of you'. To have aroused this hostility from a rival, Shakespeare must, by 1592, have been long enough in London to have made a name for himself as a playwright. We may conjecture that he had left Stratford in 1586 or 1587.

During the next twenty years, Shakespeare continued to live in London, regularly visiting his wife and family in Stratford. He continued to act, but his chief fame was as a dramatist. From 1594 he wrote exclusively for the Lord Chamberlain's Men, which rapidly became the leading dramatic company and from 1603 enjoyed the patronage of James I as the King's Men. His plays were extremely popular and he became a shareholder in his theatre company. He was able to buy lands around Stratford and a large house in the town, to which he retired about 1611. He died there on 23 April 1616 and was buried in Holy Trinity Church on 25 April.

 CHECK THE NET
You can read Shakespeare's will in his own handwriting – and in modern transcription – online at the Public Records Office: **http://www.pro.gov.uk/virtualmuseum** and search for 'Shakespeare'.

SHAKESPEARE'S DRAMATIC CAREER

Between the late 1580s and 1613 Shakespeare wrote thirty-seven plays, and contributed to some by other dramatists. This was by no means an exceptional number for a professional playwright of the times. The exact date of the composition of individual plays is a matter of debate –the date of first performance is known for only a few plays – but the broad outlines of Shakespeare's dramatic career have been established. He began in the late 1580s and early 1590s by rewriting earlier plays and working with plotlines inspired by the Classics. He concentrated on comedies (such as *The Comedy of Errors*, 1590–4, which derived from the Latin playwright Plautus) and plays dealing with English history (such as the three parts of *Henry VI*, 1589–92), though he also tried his hand at bloodthirsty revenge tragedy (*Titus Andronicus*, 1592–3, indebted to both Ovid and Seneca). During the 1590s Shakespeare developed his expertise

CHECK THE FILM

There are lots of anachronisms and inaccuracies in *Shakespeare in Love* (1998) – that's half the fun of it – but its depiction of the hand-to-mouth world of the commercial theatre has something of the energy and edginess from which Shakespeare drew his artistic power.

in these kinds of plays to write comic masterpieces such as *A Midsummer Night's Dream* (1594–5) and *As You Like It* (1599–1600) and history plays such as *Henry IV* (1596–8) and *Henry V* (1598–9).

As the new century begins a new note is detectable. Plays such as *Troilus and Cressida* (1601–2) and *Measure for Measure* (1603–4), poised between comedy and tragedy, evoke complex responses. Because of their generic uncertainty and ambivalent tone such works are sometimes referred to as 'problem plays', but it is tragedy which comes to dominate the extraordinary sequence of masterpieces: *Hamlet* (1600–1), *Othello* (1602–4), *King Lear* (1605–6), *Macbeth* (1605–6) and *Antony and Cleopatra* (1606).

In the last years of his dramatic career, Shakespeare wrote a group of plays of a quite different kind. These 'romances', as they are often called, are in many ways the most remarkable of all his plays. The group comprises *Pericles* (1608), *Cymbeline* (1609–11), *The Winter's Tale* (1610–11) and *The Tempest* (1610–11). These plays (particularly *Cymbeline*) reprise many of the situations and themes of the earlier dramas but in fantastical and exotic dramatic designs which, set in distant lands, covering large tracts of time and involving music, mime, dance and tableaux, have something of the qualities of masques and pageants. The situations which in the tragedies had led to disaster are here resolved: the great theme is restoration and reconciliation. Where in the tragedies Ophelia, Desdemona and Cordelia die, the daughters of these plays – Marina, Imogen, Perdita, Miranda – survive and are reunited with their parents and lovers.

THE TEXTS OF SHAKESPEARE'S PLAYS

Nineteen of Shakespeare's plays were printed during his lifetime in what are called 'quartos': books, each containing one play, and made up of sheets of paper each folded twice to make four leaves. Shakespeare, however, did not supervise their publication. This was not unusual. When a playwright sold a play to a dramatic company he sold his rights in it: copyright belonged to whoever had possession of an actual copy of the text, and consequently authors had no control over what happened to their work. Anyone who

CONTEXT

A quarto is a small format book, roughly equivalent to a modern paperback. Play texts in quarto form typically cost sixpence, as opposed to the cost of going to the theatre at a penny.

could get hold of the text of a play might publish it if they wished. Hence, what found its way into print might be the author's copy, but it might be an actor's copy or prompt copy, perhaps cut or altered for performance; sometimes actors (or even members of the audience) might publish what they could remember of the text. Printers, working without the benefit of the author's oversight, introduced their own errors, through misreading the manuscript for example, and by 'correcting' what seemed to them not to make sense.

In 1623 John Heminges and Henry Condell, two actors in Shakespeare's company, collected together texts of thirty-six of Shakespeare's plays (*Pericles* was omitted) and published them in a large folio (a book in which each sheet of paper is folded once in half, to give two leaves). This, the First Folio, was followed by later editions in 1632, 1663 and 1685. Despite its appearance of authority, however, the texts in the First Folio still present many difficulties, for there are printing errors and confused passages in the plays, and its texts often differ significantly from those of the earlier quartos, when these exist.

Shakespeare's texts have, then, been through a number of intermediaries. We do not have the playwright's authority for any of his plays, and hence we cannot know exactly what it was that he wrote. Bibliographers, textual critics and editors have spent a great deal of effort on endeavouring to get behind the errors, uncertainties and contradictions in the available texts to recover the plays as Shakespeare originally wrote them. What we read is the result of these efforts. Modern texts are what editors have constructed from the available evidence: they correspond to no sixteenth- or seventeenth-century editions, and to no early performance of a Shakespeare play. Furthermore, these composite texts differ from each other, for different editors read the early texts differently and come to different conclusions. A Shakespeare text is an unstable and a contrived thing.

Often, of course, its judgements embody, if not the personal prejudices of the editor, then the cultural preferences of the time in which he or she was working. Growing awareness of this has led

CONTEXT

Plays were not considered as serious literature in this period: when, in 1612, Sir Thomas Bodley was setting up his library in Oxford he instructed his staff not to buy any drama for the collection: 'haply [perhaps] some plays may be worthy the keeping, but hardly one in forty'.

 CHECK THE NET

You can find out more about the earliest editions of Shakespeare at the University of Pensylvannia's ERIC site: **http://oldsite. library.upenn.edu/ etext/collections/ furness/eric/eric. html**.

recent scholars to distrust the whole editorial enterprise and to repudiate the attempt to construct a 'perfect' text. Stanley Wells and Gary Taylor, the editors of the Oxford edition of *The Complete Works* (1988), point out that almost certainly the texts of Shakespeare's plays were altered in performance, and from one performance to another, so that there may never have been a single version. They note, too, that Shakespeare probably revised and rewrote some plays. They do not claim to print a definitive text of any play, but prefer what seems to them the 'more theatrical' version, and when there is a great difference between available versions, as with *King Lear*, they print two texts.

SHAKESPEARE AND THE ENGLISH RENAISSANCE

Shakespeare arrived in London at the very time that the Elizabethan period was poised to become the 'golden age' of English literature. Although Elizabeth reigned as queen from 1558 to 1603, the term 'Elizabethan' is used very loosely in a literary sense to refer to the period 1580 to 1625, when the great works of the age were produced. (Sometimes the later part of this period is distinguished as 'Jacobean', from the Latin form of the name of the king who succeeded Elizabeth, James I of England and VI of Scotland, who reigned from 1603 to 1625.) The poet Edmund Spenser heralded this new age with his pastoral poem *The Shepheardes Calender* (1579), and in his essay *An Apologie for Poetrie* (written about 1580, although not published until 1595) his friend Sir Philip Sidney championed the imaginative power of the 'speaking picture of poesy', famously declaring that 'Nature never set forth the earth in so rich a tapestry as divers poets have done ... Her world is brazen, the poet's only deliver a golden'.

CHECK THE NET
You can consult texts by Spenser and Sidney, and other contemporaries of Shakespeare, at Renascence Editions **http://www. uoregon.edu/ ~rbear/ren.htm**.

Spenser and Sidney were part of that rejuvenating movement in European culture which since the nineteenth century has been known by the term 'Renaissance'. Meaning literally 'rebirth' it denotes a revival and redirection of artistic and intellectual endeavour which began in Italy in the fourteenth century with the poetry of Petrarch. It spread gradually northwards across Europe, and is first detectable in England in the early sixteenth century in the writings of the scholar and statesman Sir Thomas More and in the poetry of Sir Thomas Wyatt and Henry Howard, Earl of Surrey. Its keynote was a curiosity in thought which challenged old assumptions and traditions. To the innovative spirit of the Renaissance, the preceding ages appeared dully unoriginal and conformist.

That spirit was fuelled by the rediscovery of many Classical texts and the culture of Greece and Rome. This fostered a confidence in human reason and in human potential which, in every sphere, challenged old convictions. The discovery of America and its peoples (Columbus had sailed in 1492) demonstrated that the world was a larger and stranger place than had been thought. The cosmological speculation of Copernicus (later confirmed by Galileo) that the sun, not the earth was the centre of our planetary system challenged the centuries-old belief that the earth and human beings were at the centre of the cosmos. The pragmatic political philosophy of Machiavelli seemed to cut politics free from its traditional link with morality by permitting to statesmen any means that secured the desired end. And the religious movements we know collectively as the Reformation broke with the Church of Rome and set the individual conscience, not ecclesiastical authority, at the centre of the religious life. Nothing, it seemed, was beyond questioning, nothing impossible.

Shakespeare's drama is innovative and challenging in exactly the way of the Renaissance. It examines and questions the beliefs, assumptions and politics upon which Elizabethan society was founded. And although the plays always conclude in a restoration of order and stability, many critics are inclined to argue that their imaginative energy goes into subverting, rather than reinforcing, traditional values. Frequently, figures of authority are undercut by some comic or parodic figure: against the Duke in *Measure for Measure* is set Lucio; against Prospero in *The Tempest*, Caliban; against Henry IV, Falstaff. Despairing, critical, dissident, disillusioned, unbalanced, rebellious, mocking voices are repeatedly to be heard in the plays, rejecting, resenting, defying the established order. They belong always to marginal, socially unacceptable figures, 'licensed', as it were, by their situations to say what would be unacceptable from socially privileged or responsible citizens. The

CHECK THE NET
The Luminarium site has links to a wide range of historical information on sixteenth-century topics including astronomy, medicine, economics and technology: **http://www.luminarium.org**.

question is: are such characters given these views to discredit them, or were they the only ones through whom a voice could be given to radical and dissident ideas? Was Shakespeare a conservative or a revolutionary?

Renaissance culture was intensely nationalistic. With the break-up of the internationalism of the Middle Ages the evolving nation states which still mark the map of Europe began for the first time to acquire distinctive cultural identities. There was intense rivalry among them as they sought to achieve, in their own vernacular languages, a culture that could equal that of Greece and Rome. Spenser's great allegorical epic poem *The Faerie Queene*, which began to appear from 1590, celebrated Elizabeth and was intended to outdo the poetic achievements of France and Italy and to stand beside the works of Virgil and Homer. Shakespeare is equally preoccupied with national identity. His history plays tell an epic story that examines how modern England came into being through the conflicts of the fifteenth-century Wars of the Roses which brought the Tudors to the throne. He is fascinated, too, by the related subject of politics and the exercise of power. With the collapse of medieval feudalism and the authority of local barons, the royal court in the Renaissance came to assume a new status as the centre of power and patronage. It was here that the destiny of a country was shaped. Courts, and how to succeed in them, consequently fascinated the Renaissance; and they fascinated Shakespeare and his audience.

But the dramatic gaze is not merely admiring; through a variety of devices, a critical perspective is brought to bear. The court may be paralleled by a very different world, revealing uncomfortable similarities (for example, Henry's court and the Boar's Head tavern, ruled over by Falstaff in *Henry IV*). Its hypocrisy may be bitterly denounced (for example, in the diatribes of the mad Lear) and its self-seeking ambition represented disturbingly in the figure of a Machiavellian villain (such as Edmund in *Lear*) or a malcontent (such as Iago in *Othello*). Shakespeare is fond of displacing the court to another context, the better to examine its assumptions and pretensions and to offer alternatives to the courtly life (for example, in the pastoral setting of the forest of Arden in *As You Like It* or

CHECK THE BOOK

Benedict Anderson's book on the rise of the nation and nationalism, *Imagined Communities* (revised ed., 1991), has been influential for its definition of the nation as 'an imagined political community' – imagined in part through cultural productions such as Shakespeare's history plays.

Prospero's island in *The Tempest*). Courtiers are frequently figures of fun whose unmanly sophistication ('neat and trimly dressed, / Fresh as a bridegroom ... perfumed like a milliner', says Hotspur of such a man in *1 Henry IV*, I.3.33–6) is contrasted with plain-speaking integrity: Oswald is set against Kent in *King Lear*.

When thinking of these matters, we should remember that stage plays were subject to censorship, and any criticism had therefore to be muted or oblique: direct criticism of the monarch or contemporary English court would not be tolerated. This has something to do with why Shakespeare's plays are always set either in the past, or abroad.

The nationalism of the English Renaissance was reinforced by Protestantism. Henry VIII had broken with Rome in the 1530s and in Shakespeare's time there was an independent Protestant state church. Because the Pope in Rome had excommunicated Queen Elizabeth as a heretic and relieved the English of their allegiance to the crown, there was deep suspicion of Roman Catholics as potential traitors. This was enforced by the attempted invasion of the Spanish Armada in 1588. This was a religiously inspired crusade to overthrow Elizabeth and restore England to Roman Catholic allegiance. Roman Catholicism was hence easily identified with hostility to England. Its association with disloyalty and treachery was then reinforced by the Gunpowder Plot of 1605, a Roman Catholic attempt to destroy the government of England.

Shakespeare's plays are remarkably free from direct religious sentiment, but their emphases are Protestant. Young women, for example, are destined for marriage, not for nunneries (precisely what Isabella appears to escape at the end of *Measure for Measure*); friars are dubious characters, full of schemes and deceptions, if with benign intentions, as in *Much Ado About Nothing* or *Romeo and Juliet*. (We should add that Puritans, extreme Protestants, are even less kindly treated than Roman Catholics: for example, Malvolio in *Twelfth Night*).

The central figures of the plays are frequently individuals beset by temptation, by the lure of evil – Angelo in *Measure for Measure*,

CHECK THE FILM
We can get a modern equivalent of the effect of this displacement from Christine Edzard's film of *As You Like It* (1992). Here, the court scenes are set in the luxurious headquarters of a bank or company; the woodland scenes amid a sort of 'cardboard city' of social outcasts and the vulnerable.

Othello, Lear, Macbeth – and not only in tragedies: Falstaff is described as 'that old white-bearded Satan' (*1 Henry IV*, II.4.454). We follow their inner struggles. Shakespeare's heroes have the preoccupation with self and the introspective tendencies encouraged by Protestantism: his tragic heroes are haunted by their consciences, seeking their true selves, agonising over what course of action to take as they follow what can often be understood as a kind of spiritual progress towards heaven or hell.

SHAKESPEARE'S THEATRE

CHECK THE NET
Find out more about the Shakespearean theatre at **http://www.reading.ac.uk/globe**. This web site describes the historical researches undertaken in connection with the Globe theatre on London's Bankside, which was rebuilt in the late 1990s.

The theatre for which the plays were written was one of the most remarkable innovations of the Renaissance. There had been no theatres or acting companies during the medieval period. Performed on carts and in open spaces at Christian festivals, plays had been almost exclusively religious. Such professional actors as there were wandered the country putting on a variety of entertainments in the yards of inns, on makeshift stages in market squares, or anywhere else suitable. They did not perform full-length plays, but mimes, juggling and comedy acts. Such actors were regarded by officialdom and polite society as little better than vagabonds and layabouts.

Just before Shakespeare went to London all this began to change. A number of young men who had been to the universities of Oxford and Cambridge came to London in the 1580s and began to write plays that made use of what they had learned about the classical drama of ancient Greece and Rome. Plays such as John Lyly's *Alexander and Campaspe* (1584), Christopher Marlowe's *Tamburlaine the Great* (about 1587) and Thomas Kyd's *The Spanish Tragedy* (1588–9) were unlike anything that had been written in English before. They were full-length plays on secular subjects, taking their plots from history and legend, adopting many of the devices of Classical drama, and offering a range of characterisation and situation hitherto unattempted in English drama. With the exception of Lyly's prose dramas, they were composed in the unrhymed iambic pentameters (blank verse), which the Earl of Surrey had introduced into English earlier in the sixteenth century. This was a freer and more expressive medium than the rhymed verse of medieval drama. It was the drama of these 'university wits' that Shakespeare challenged when he came to London. Greene was one of them, and we have heard how little he liked Shakespeare setting himself up as a dramatist.

The most significant change of all, however, was that these dramatists wrote for the professional theatre. In 1576 James Burbage built the first permanent theatre in England, in Shoreditch, just beyond London's northern boundary. It was called simply 'The Theatre'. Others soon followed. Thus, when Shakespeare came to London, there was a flourishing drama, theatres and companies of actors waiting for him, such as there had never been before in England. His company performed at James Burbage's Theatre until 1596, and used the Swan and Curtain until they moved into their own new theatre, the Globe, in 1599. It was burned down in 1613 when a cannon was fired during a performance of Shakespeare's *Henry VIII*.

With the completion in 1996 of Sam Wanamaker's project to construct in London a replica of the Globe, and with productions now running there, a version of Shakespeare's theatre can be experienced at first hand. It is very different to the usual modern experience of drama. The form of the Elizabethan theatre derived from the inn yards and animal baiting rings in which actors had been accustomed to perform in the past. They were circular wooden buildings with a paved courtyard in the middle open to the sky. A rectangular stage jutted out into the middle of this yard. Some of the audience stood in the yard (or 'pit') to watch the play. They were thus on three sides of the stage, close up to it and on a level with it. These 'groundlings' paid only a penny to get in, but for wealthier spectators there were seats in three covered tiers or galleries between the inner and outer walls of the building, extending round most of the auditorium and overlooking the pit and the stage. Such a theatre could hold about 3,000 spectators. The yards were about 80ft in diameter and the rectangular stage approximately 40ft by 30ft and 5ft 6in high. Shakespeare aptly called such a theatre a 'wooden O' in the prologue to *Henry V* (line 13).

The stage itself was partially covered by a roof or canopy, which projected from the wall at the rear of the stage and was supported

CHECK THE BOOK

The most authoritative book on what we know about the theatre of Shakespeare's time is Andrew Gurr's *The Shakespearean Stage* (1992).

CONTEXT

Whereas now, we would conceptualise a visit to the theatre as going to *see* a play, the most common Elizabethan phrase was 'to go *hear* a play' (as in *The Taming of the Shrew*, Induction 2.130) – thus registering the different sensory priorities of the early modern theatre.

THE GLOBE THEATRE,

On the ... Bankside.

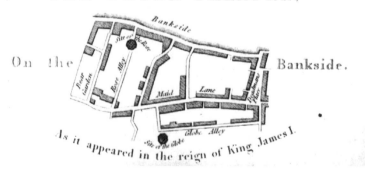

As it appeared in the reign of King James I.

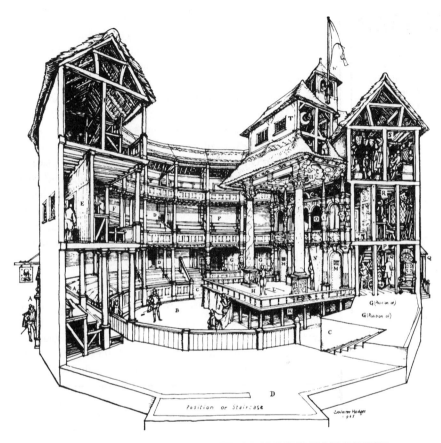

A CONJECTURAL RECONSTRUCTION OF THE INTERIOR OF THE GLOBE PLAYHOUSE

AA   Main entrance

B   The Yard

CC   Entrances to lowest galleries

D   Entrance to staircase and upper galleries

E   Corridor serving the different sections of the middle gallery

F   Middle gallery ('Twopenny Rooms')

G   'Gentlemen's Rooms or Lords Rooms'

H   The stage

J   The hanging being put up round the stage

K   The 'Hell' under the stage

L   The stage trap, leading down to the Hell

MM   Stage doors

N   Curtained 'place behind the stage'

O   Gallery above the stage, used as required sometimes by musicians, sometimes by spectators, and often as part of the play

P   Back-stage area (the tiring-house)

Q   Tiring-house door

R   Dressing-rooms

S   Wardrobe and storage

T   The hut housing the machine for lowering enthroned gods, etc., to the stage

U   The 'Heavens'

W   Hoisting the playhouse flag

CONTEXT

We do not know much about the props list for a theatre company in Shakespeare's time, although the evidence we do have suggests that there were some quite ambitious examples: one list dating from 1598 includes decorated cloths depicting cities or the night sky, items of armour, horses' heads and 'one hell mouth', probably for performances of Marlowe's famous play *Doctor Faustus*.

by two posts at the front. This protected the stage and performers from inclement weather, and to it were secured winches and other machinery for stage effects. On either side at the back of the stage was a door. These led into the dressing room (or 'tiring house') and it was by means of these doors that actors entered and left the stage. Between these doors was a small recess or alcove which was curtained off. Such a 'discovery place' served, for example, for Juliet's bedroom when in Act IV Scene 4 of *Romeo and Juliet* the Nurse went to the back of the stage and drew the curtain to find Juliet apparently dead on her bed. Above the discovery place was a balcony, used for the famous balcony scenes of *Romeo and Juliet* (II.2 and III.5), or for the battlements of Richard's castle when he is confronted by Bolingbroke in *Richard II* (III.3). Actors (all parts in the Elizabethan theatre were taken by boys or men) had access to the area beneath the stage; from here, in the 'cellarage', would have come the voice of the ghost of Hamlet's father (*Hamlet*, II.1.150–82).

On these stages there was very little in the way of scenery or props – there was nowhere to store them (there were no wings in this theatre) nor any way to set them up (no tabs across the stage), and, anyway, productions had to be transportable for performance at court or at noble houses. The stage was bare, which is why characters often tell us where they are: there was nothing on the stage to indicate location. It is also why location is so rarely topographical, and much more often symbolic. It suggests a dramatic mood or situation, rather than a place: Lear's barren heath reflects his destitute state, as the storm his emotional turmoil.

None of the plays printed in Shakespeare's lifetime marks act or scene divisions. These have been introduced by later editors, but they should not mislead us into supposing that there was any break in Elizabethan performances such as might happen today while the curtains are closed and the set is changed. The staging of Elizabethan plays was continuous, with the many short 'scenes' of which Shakespeare's plays are often constructed following one after another in quick succession. We have to think of a more fluid, and much faster, production than we are generally used to: in the prologues to *Romeo and Juliet* (line 12) and *Henry VIII* (line 13)

Shakespeare speaks of the playing time as only two hours. It is because plays were staged continuously that exits and entrances are written in as part of the script: characters speak as they enter or leave the stage because otherwise there would be a silence while, in full view, they took up their positions. (This is also why dead bodies have to be carried off: they cannot get up and walk off.)

In 1608 Shakespeare's company, the King's Men, acquired the Blackfriars Theatre, a smaller, rectangular indoor theatre, holding about 700 people, with seats for all the members of the audience, facilities for elaborate stage effects and, because it was enclosed, artificial lighting. It has been suggested that the plays written for this 'private' theatre differed from those written for the Globe, since, as it cost more to go to a private theatre, the audience came from a higher social stratum and demanded the more elaborate and courtly entertainment which Shakespeare's romances provide. However, the King's Men continued to play at the Globe in the summer, using Blackfriars in the winter, and it is not certain that Shakespeare's last plays were written specifically for the Blackfriars theatre, or first performed there.

READING SHAKESPEARE

Shakespeare's plays were written for this stage, but there is also a sense in which they were written *by* the stage. The material and physical circumstances of their production in such theatres had a profound effect upon the nature of Elizabethan plays. Unless we bear this in mind, we are likely to find them very strange, for we will read with expectations shaped by our own familiarity with modern fiction and modern drama which is, by and large, realistic; it seeks to persuade us that what we are reading or watching is really happening. This is quite foreign to Shakespeare. If we try to read him like this, we shall find ourselves irritated by the improbabilities of his plot, confused by his chronology, puzzled by locations, frustrated by unanswered questions and dissatisfied by the motivation of the action. The absurd ease with which disguised persons pass through Shakespeare's plays is a case in point: why does no one recognise people they know so well? There is a great deal of psychological accuracy in Shakespeare's plays, but we are far from any attempt at realism.

 CHECK THE BOOK
Deborah Cartmell's *Interpreting Shakespeare on Screen* (2000) is recommended for its clear and interesting sense of the possibilities and the requirements of approaching Shakespeare through the cinema.

CONTEXT

The Romantic critic S. T. Coleridge argued that literature requires our 'willing suspension of disbelief': but it is not clear that the theatre of the Shakespearean period did require its audience to forget that they were in a theatre. Certainly, remarks calling attention to the theatrical setting are commonplace – in comedies such as *Twelfth Night* (III.4.125) and *As You Like It* II.7.139–43, and in tragedies including *Macbeth* (V.5.23–5) – making it more difficult to forget the theatricality of the stories depicted.

The reason is that in Shakespeare's theatre it was impossible to pretend that the audience was not watching a contrived performance. In a modern theatre, the audience is encouraged to forget itself as it becomes absorbed by the action on stage. The worlds of the spectators and of the actors are sharply distinguished by the lighting: in the dark auditorium the audience is passive, silent, anonymous, receptive and attentive; on the lighted stage the actors are active, vocal, demonstrative and dramatic. (The distinction is, of course, still more marked in the cinema.) There is no communication between the two worlds: for the audience to speak would be interruptive; for the actors to address the audience would be to break the illusion of the play. In the Elizabethan theatre, this distinction did not exist, and for two reasons: first, performances took place in the open air and in daylight which illuminated everyone equally; secondly, the spectators were all around the stage (and wealthier spectators actually on it), and were dressed no differently from the actors, who wore contemporary dress. In such a theatre, spectators would be as aware of each other as of the actors; they could not lose their identity in a corporate group, nor could they ever forget that they were spectators at a performance. There was no chance that they could believe 'this is really happening'.

This, then, was communal theatre, not only in the sense that it was going on in the middle of a crowd but also in the sense that the crowd joined in. Elizabethan audiences had none of our deference: they did not keep quiet, nor arrive on time, nor remain for the whole performance. They joined in, interrupted, even getting on the stage. And plays were preceded and followed by jigs and clowning. It was all much more like our experience of a pantomime, and at a pantomime we are fully aware, and are meant to be aware, that we are watching games being played with reality. The conventions of pantomime revel in their own artificiality: the fishnet tights are to signal that the handsome prince is a woman, the Dame's monstrous false breasts signal that 'she' is a man.

Something very similar is the case with Elizabethan theatre: it utilised its very theatricality. Instead of trying to persuade spectators that they are not in a theatre watching a performance,

Elizabethan plays acknowledge the presence of the audience. It is addressed not only by prologues, epilogues and choruses, but also in soliloquies. There is no realistic reason why characters should suddenly explain themselves to empty rooms, but, of course, there is no empty room. The actor is surrounded by people. Soliloquies are not addressed to the world of the play; they are for the audience's benefit. And that audience's complicity is assumed: when a character like Prospero declares himself to be invisible, it is accepted that he is. Disguises are taken to be impenetrable, however improbable, and we are to accept impossibly contrived situations, such as barely hidden characters remaining undetected (indeed, on the Elizabethan stage there was nowhere at all they could hide).

These, then, are plays that are aware of themselves as dramas; in critical terminology, they are self-reflexive, commenting upon themselves as dramatic pieces and prompting the audience to think about the theatrical experience. They do this not only through their direct address to the audience but also through their fondness for the play-within-a-play (which reminds the audience that the encompassing play is also a play) and their constant use of images from, and allusions to, the theatre. They are fascinated by role-playing, by acting, appearance and reality. Things are rarely what they seem, either in comedy (for example, in *A Midsummer Night's Dream*) or tragedy (*Romeo and Juliet*). This offers one way to think about those disguises: they are thematic rather than realistic. Kent's disguise in *Lear* reveals his true, loyal self, while Edmund, who is not disguised, hides his true self. In *As You Like It*, Rosalind is more truly herself disguised as a man than when dressed as a woman.

The effect of all this is to confuse the distinction we would make between 'real life' and 'acting'. The case of Rosalind, for example, raises searching questions about gender roles, about how far it is 'natural' to be womanly or manly: how does the stage, on which a man can play a woman playing a man (and have a man fall in love with him/her), differ from life, in which we assume the roles we think appropriate to masculine and feminine behaviour? The same is true of political roles: when a Richard II or Lear is so aware of the regal part he is performing, of the trappings and rituals of kingship,

CHECK THE NET

The 'Designing Shakespeare' database at PADS (**www.pads.ahds. ac.uk**) has an extensive collection of photographs from different productions available online.

CONTEXT

The poet Walter Raleigh wrote a poem on this image of life as theatre, which begins 'What is our life? A play of passion', in which 'our mothers' wombs the tiring houses be / When we are dressed for this short comedy'. There's a twist at the end of the short verse: 'only we die in earnest, that's no jest'.

their plays raise the uncomfortable possibility that the answer to the question of what constitutes a successful king is simply: a good actor. Indeed, human life generally is repeatedly rendered through the imagery of the stage, from Macbeth's 'Life's but a walking shadow, a poor player / That struts and frets his hour upon the stage / And then is heard no more' (V.5.23–5) to Prospero's paralleling of human life to a performance which, like the globe (both world and theatre!) will end (IV.I.146–58). When life is a fiction, like this play, or this play is a fiction like life, what is the difference? 'All the world's a stage...' (*As You Like It*, II.7.139).

World events	Shakespeare's life *(dates for plays are approximate)*	Literature and the arts
1559 Coronation of Elizabeth I		
	1564 Born in Stratford-upon-Avon	
1577 Francis Drake leaves Plymouth aboard *Pelican* to sail round the world, returning in 1580		
1582 Outbreak of the plague in London	**1582** Marries Anne Hathaway	
	1583 His daughter, Susanna, is born	
	1585 His twins, Hamnet and Judith, are born	
1587 Mary Queen of Scots is executed		**1587** Christopher Marlowe, *Tamburlaine the Great*
		1590 Edmund Spenser, *The Faerie Queen*
1592 The plague in London leads to the closing of theatres until 1594	**1592** Writes *The Comedy of Errors*	**1592** Christopher Marlowe, *Doctor Faustus*
	1593 *Richard III, The Two Gentlemen of Verona* and *Titus Andronicus*	**1593** Christopher Marlowe is killed in tavern brawl at Deptford
	1594 *The Taming of the Shrew*	
	1595 *Love's Labours Lost, Romeo and Juliet,* and *A Midsummer Night's Dream*	**1595** Montaigne, *Essais*
	1596 Hamnet dies. *The Merchant of Venice*	
	1597 *Henry IV Parts I and II*	
1598 Death of King Phillip II of Spain	**1598** *Much Ado About Nothing*	**1598** Ben Johnson, *Every Man in his Humour*
	1599 Globe Theatre opens in London. *Julius Caesar, Henry V* and *As You Like It*	
	1600 *The Merry Wives of Windsor* and *Twelfth Night*	
1601 Poor Law Act passed by Parliament	**1601** *Hamlet*	**1601** John Marston, *What You Will*
	1602 *Troilus and Cressida* and *All's Well That Ends Well*	

continued

World events	Shakespeare's life	Literature and the arts
	(dates for plays are approximate)	
1603 Death of Elizabeth I, and accession of James I	**1603** A garbled pirated edition of Hamlet comes out (First Quarto). Shakespeare's company is granted a royal patent by James I	
1604 Hampton Court Conference agrees a new 'authorised' translation of the Bible is needed	**1604** *Othello* and *Measure for Measure*	
1605 The Gunpowder plot – Guy Fawkes is arrested while preparing explosives in the cellar of the Palace of Westminster	**1605** *King Lear*. An authorised version of *Hamlet*, which the printer claimed to be 'according to the true and perfect copy' (Second Quarto), is published	**1605** Miguel de Cervantes Saavedra, Spanish novelist, *Don Quixote*
1606 James I proclaims a national flag ('Union Jack') that combines the St George's cross and St Andrews saltire	**1606** *Macbeth* and *Antony and Cleopatra*	**1606** Ben Johnson, *Volpone*
	1607 *Timon of Athens*	
	1608 *Coriolanus* and *Pericles*	
	1609 *Cymbeline* and *Sonnets*	
	1610 *The Winter's Tale*	
1611 Authorised Version of the Bible is published	**1611** *The Tempest*	
	1613 Globe Theatre burns down; reopens 1614	
		1614 John Webster, *The Duchess of Malfi*
	1616 William Shakespeare dies	**1616** Inigo Jones designs the Queen's House, Greenwich
1620 A group of settlers, later to be called the Pilgrim Fathers, set sail in the *Mayflower* for the New World		
	1623 A collection of all Shakespeare's plays is printed (First Folio), in which the text of Hamlet is significantly different from the two earlier texts	
1625 James I dies, and is succeeded by Charles I		

More has been written about *Hamlet* than about any other work of literature. The typical college library would not be large enough to house all the books and articles that have been written about the play, about its principal characters and themes, and about *Hamlet* criticism itself.

We list here, therefore, only a handful of studies that have excited over a long period a great deal of response, together with some suggestions for those who wish to explore the directions in which *Hamlet* criticism has been moving recently.

CRITICAL STUDIES

J. Dryden, *Preface to Troilus & Cressida,* 1679

Samuel Johnson, *Preface to Shakespeare; Notes on Hamlet,* 1765

Johann Wolfgang Goethe, *Wilhelm Meister's Apprenticeship,* 1796

William Richardson, *Some of Shakespeare's Remarkable Characters,* 1783

Samuel Coleridge, *Lecture and Notes on Hamlet,* 1811–12, 1813, 1818

Anna Brownell Jameson, *Characteristics of Shakespeare's Women,* 1832

Herman Ulrici, *Shakespeare's Dramatic Art,* 1839

Victor Hugo, *William Shakespeare,* 1864

Sir Sidney Lee, *A Life of William Shakespeare,* 1898

A. C. Bradley, *Shakespearean Tragedy,* Macmillan, 1904

T. S. Eliot, 'Hamlet and His Problems', in *The Sacred Wood: Essays on Poetry and Criticism,* Faber, 1922

Harley Granville-Barker, *Preface to Hamlet,* Batsford, 1930

G. Wilson Knight, *The Wheel of Fire,* Oxford University Press, 1930

G. Wilson Knight, *The Imperial Theme,* Oxford University Press, 1931

A. J. A. Waldock, *Hamlet: A Study in Critical Method,* Cambridge University Press, 1931

John Dover Wilson, *What Happens in Hamlet,* Cambridge University Press, 1935

Caroline Spurgeon, *Shakespeare's Imagery and What It Tells Us,* Cambridge University Press, 1935

H. A. Saintsbury and Cecil Palmer (eds.), *We Saw Him Act,* 1939

L. L. Schücking, *The Meaning of Hamlet*, Doubleday, 1939

Ernst Jones, *Hamlet and Oedipus*, Victor Gollancz Ltd., 1949

W. H. Clemen, *The Development of Shakespeare's Imagery*, Harvard University Press, 1951

William Empson, 'Hamlet When New' (1953) in (ed.) David Pirie *Essays on Shakespeare*, Cambridge University Press, 1986

M. M. Mahood, *Shakespeare's Wordplay*, Methuen, 1957

T. S. Eliot, *On Poetry and Poets*, Faber, 1957

L. C. Knights, *An Approach to Hamlet*, Chatto & Windus, 1960

Jan Kott, *Shakespeare Our Contemporary*, Doubleday, 1964

Brecht on Theatre, tr. John Willett, Methuen, 1964

Morris Weitz, *Hamlet and the Philosophy of Literary Criticism*, Faber, 1965

Eleanor Prosser, *Hamlet and Revenge*, Stanford University Press, 1967

John Jump (ed.), *Hamlet Casebook*, Macmillan, 1968

Walter N. King, *Hamlet's Search for Meaning*, University of Georgia Press, 1982

James L. Calderwood, *To Be And Not To Be, Negation and Metadrama in Hamlet*, Columbia University Press, 1983

Catherine Belsey, *The Subject of Tragedy*, Methuen, 1985

Terry Eagleton, *William Shakespeare*, Basil Blackwell, 1986

L. Tennenhouse, *Power on Display: The Politics of Shakespeare's Genres*, Methuen, 1986

Michael Hattaway, *Hamlet: The Critics Debate*, Macmillan, 1987

Peter Mercer, *Hamlet and the Acting of Revenge*, Macmillan, 1987

Kenneth S. Rothwell and Annabelle Henkin Melzer, *Shakespeare on Screen: An International Filmography and Videography*, Neal-Schuman Publishers, Inc., 1990

Alex Newell *The soliloquies in Hamlet: the structural design*, Associated University Presses, 1991

Martin Coyle, *Hamlet: New Casebooks*, Macmillan, 1992

Anthony Davies and Stanley Wells (eds.), *Shakespeare and the Moving Image*, Cambridge University Press, 1994

Jonathan Dollimore and Alan Sinfield (eds.), *Political Shakespeare, Essays in Cultural Materialism*, Manchester University Press, second edition, 1994

Elizabeth Oakes, 'Polonius, The Man Behind the Arras', in (eds.) Mark Thornton Burnett and John Manning, *New Essays on Hamlet*, AMS Press, New York, 1994

Kay Stanton, 'Hamlet's Whores', in (eds.) Mark Thornton Burnett and John Manning, *New Essays on Hamlet*, AMS Press, New York, 1994

John Russell, *Hamlet and Narcissus*, University of Delaware Press, 1995

George T. Wright, 'Hendiadys and *Hamlet*' in (eds.) David Scott Kastan, , *Critical Essays on Shakespeare's Hamlet,* G. K. Hall and Co., 1995

Victor Kiernan, *Eight tragedies of Shakespeare, A Marxist Study*, Verso, 1996

Michael Pennington, *Hamlet: A User's Guide* Nick Hern, 1996

Kenneth Branagh, *Hamlet by William Shakespeare: Screenplay & Introduction*, Chatto & Windus, 1996

Lisa Jardine, *Reading Shakespeare Historically*, Routledge, 1996

John Adler (ed.), *Responses to Shakespeare* (8 volumes), Routledge, 1997

Stanley Wells, *Shakespeare in the Theatre, An Anthology of Criticism,* Oxford University Press, 1997

K. Parsons and P. Mason, *Shakespeare in Performance*, Salamander Books, 1997

Lynda E. Boose and Richard Burt (eds.), *Shakespeare the Movie*, Routledge, 1997

Anthony B Dawson, *Shakespeare in Performance: Hamlet*, Manchester University Press, 1997

Holger Klein and Dimiter Daphinoff (eds.), *Hamlet on Screen*, Edwin Mellen Press, 1997

Maurice Charney, *Hamlet's Fictions*, Routledge, 1998

Karin S. Coddon, ' "Suche strange desygns", Madness, Subjectivity and Treason in *Hamlet* and Elizabethan Culture', reprinted in (ed.) Susan Zimmerman, *New Casebooks, Shakespeare's Tragedies*, Methuen, 1998

Michael D. Bristol, ' "Funeral Bak'd meats": Carnival and the Carnivalesque in Hamlet', reprinted in (ed.) Susan Zimmerman, *New Casebooks, Shakespeare's Tragedies*, Methuen, 1998

Robert Shaughnessy (ed.), *Shakespeare on Film: New Casebooks*, Macmillan, 1998

David Farley-Hills, *Critical Responses to Hamlet 1600–1854* (three volumes), AMS Press New York, 1996–9

Robert Hapgood (ed.), *Shakespeare in Production: Hamlet*, Cambridge University Press, 1999

Lisa S. Starks, 'The displaced body of desire: Sexuality in Kenneth Branagh's *Hamlet*', in (eds.) Christy Desmet and Robert Sawyer, *Shakespeare and Appropriation*, Routledge, 1999

Linda Charnes, 'We were never early modern' in (ed.) John J. Joughin, *Philosophical Shakespeares*, Routledge, 2000

Andrew Gurr and Mariko Ichikawa, *Staging In Shakespeare's Theatres*, Oxford University Press, 2000

Robert Shaughnessy (ed.), *Shakespeare in Performance*, Palgrave, 2000

Russell Jackson (ed.) *The Cambridge Companion to Shakespeare on Film*, Cambridge University Press, 2000

Frank Kermode, *Shakespeare's Language* , Allen Lane, Penguin, 2000

Peter Stallybrass, '*Well grubbed, old mole*', Marx, *Hamlet* and the (un)fixing of Representation' in (eds.) Jean E. Howard and Scott Cutler Shershow, *Marxist Shakespeares*, Routledge, 2001

Philip Armstrong, *Shakespeare In Psychoanalysis*, Routledge, 2001

Stephen Greenblatt, *Hamlet in Purgatory*, Princeton, 2001

Jonathan Bate and Russell Jackson, *The Oxford Illustrated History of Shakespeare on Stage*, Oxford University Press, 2001

Alexander Welsh, *Hamlet in his modern guises*, Princeton University Press, 2001

A website dedicated to recent developments in *Hamlet* criticism will be found at:
http://helios.acomp.usf.edu/~sjenkin3/loberg/haven.html

EDITIONS OF *HAMLET*

Kathleen O. Irace, (ed.), *The First Quarto of Hamlet*, Cambridge University Press, 1998

Peter Alexander (ed.), *The Works of Shakespeare*, Collins, 1951

C. Hinman (ed.), *The First Folio of Shakespeare*, Norton, 1968, 1996

Harold Jenkins (ed.), *Hamlet: The Arden Shakespeare*, Methuen, 1982

Philip Edwards (ed.), *Hamlet: The New Cambridge Shakespeare,* Cambridge University Press, 1985

G.R. Hibbard (ed.), *Hamlet: The Oxford Shakespeare,* Oxford University Press, 1987

Paul Bertram and Bernice W. Kliman, (eds.), *The Three Text Hamlet,* AMS Press, 1991
   Presents the three earliest versions of the play (Q1, Q2 & F1) side by side

Richard Andrews and Rex Gibson (eds.), *Hamlet: The Cambridge School Shakespeare,* Cambridge University Press, 1994

Blakemore Evans and others, (eds.) *The Riverside Shakespeare, Second Edition,* Houghton Mifflin Company, Boston/New York, 1997

S. Greenblatt and others (eds.) *The Norton Shakespeare,* Norton, 1997

FILMS OF *HAMLET*

Dozens of films have been made of *Hamlet*. There is even a silent, five-minute one of Sarah Bernhardt playing the Prince, dating from 1900. Their availability is always uncertain but with the advent of DVD, many interesting productions from the past are being restored to the catalogue.

You may find some of the films we recommend below temporarily 'out of print' but available on VHS from your local library or teachers' centre. We have selected the handful below for the exciting ways they engage with Shakespeare's text. As we have suggested in the commentaries, it is particularly rewarding to compare the way key scenes are presented in several different productions. If you are able to watch only two productions, the Kozinstev and Bennett are highly recommended.

Hamlet (Denmark, 1920) Directors: Svena Gade and Heinz Schall. Asta Nielsen as Hamlet

Hamlet (UK, 1948) Director: Laurence Olivier. Laurence Olivier as Hamlet

Hamlet (USA, 1960) Director: Franz Peter Wirth. Maximilian Schell as Hamlet

Hamlet (USSR, 1964) Director: Grigori Kozinstev. Innokenti Smoktunovski as Hamlet

Hamlet (USA, 1964) Directors: Bill Colleran & John Gielgud. Richard Burton as Hamlet

Hamlet (UK, 1969) Director: Tony Richardson. Nicol Williamson as Hamlet

Hamlet (UK, 1980) Director: Rodney Bennett. Derek Jacobi as Hamlet

Hamlet (UK, 1990) Director: Franco Zeffirelli. Mel Gibson as Hamlet

Rosencrantz and Guildenstern are Dead (US, 1990) Director: Tom Stoppard

Hamlet: The Animated Tales (UK, 1992) Director: Natalia Orlova

Hamlet (UK, 1996) Director: Kenneth Branagh. Kenneth Branagh as Hamlet

Hamlet (USA, 2000) Director: Michael Almereyda. Ethan Hawke as Hamlet

We urge all students to see at least one live production of the play, even a workshop production; nothing on film can convey the electricity of the actors' direct communication with an audience.

AUDIOBOOKS OF *HAMLET*

Shakespeare's richly musical language works on the imagination. It is much easier to understand, enjoy and respond to *Hamlet* if you hear it performed by expert actors rather than try to read it silently to yourself. There are many excellent audiobooks of *Hamlet* available on CD and cassette. The following can be strongly recommended:

Random House Audiobooks: Kennneth Branagh as Hamlet

HarperCollins: Paul Scofield as Hamlet

Naxos: Anton Lesser as Hamlet

If you have access to the Internet, you may find the cheapest way of acquiring a complete recording of the play is to download one directly onto your computer.

blank verse rhythmically regular verse which does not rhyme. Shakespeare's blank verse is written in what is known as 'iambic pentameter' because each ten syllable line consists of five 'iambs', one unstressed followed by one stressed syllable:

```
   x    /   x    /   x    /    x    /   x     /
Though  yet  of  Hamlet  our  dear  brother's  death  (I.2.1)
```

In Shakespeare's early plays, the verse is very regular. Often each line is rhythmically 'complete' in itself as the punctuation suggests:

> Let's raise the siege; why live we idly here?
> Talbot is taken, whom we wont to fear;
> Remaineth none but mad-brain'd Salisbury,
> And he may well in fretting spend his gall-
> Nor men nor money hath he to make war.   (1 Henry VI, I.2.13–17)

As his technique developed, so Shakespeare's verse became increasingly rhythmically flexible, able to accommodate fluctuating changes of mood:

> Am I a coward?
> Who calls me villain, breaks my pate across,
> Plucks off my beard and blows it in my face,
> Tweaks me by the'nose, gives me the lie i'the'throat
> As deep as to the lungs? Who does me this?
> Ha, 'swounds, I should take it, for it cannot be
> But I am pigeon-livered, and lack gall
> To make oppression bitter, or ere this
> I should ha' fatted all the region kites
> With this slave's offal. Bloody, bawdy, villain!
> Oh, vengeance!   (II.2.523–34)

Shakespeare maintains the strength of the regularity of verse here. The dramatic energy and the illusion that this is natural speech comes from the way he mixes regular ten-syllable lines with lines of irregular length, and from the way the punctuation often straddles the lines of verse, an idea running on from one line to the next (enjambement) as here:

> gives me the lie i'the'throat
> As deep as to the lungs?

and then pauses in the middle of a line (caesura). This freeing of rhythm from the straight-jacket of regular iambic pentameter was something which continued to develop to the end of Shakespeare's career

chorus in the tragedies of the ancient Greek playwrights, Aeschylus and Sophocles, the 'chorus' is a group of characters who represent ordinary people in their attitudes to the action, which they witness as bystanders, and on which they comment. In Shakespeare's plays, however, the Chorus acts as a narrator, giving the audience information there is not stage time enough to dramatise.

Folio a large page size, formed by a single fold in a sheet of printer's paper, giving four pages (or sides). Shakespeare's plays were first collected by Heminge and Condell in the volume called the First Folio in 1623. Before this, only nineteen of his plays had been published in unauthorised **Quarto** editions

Hendiadys a rhetorical figure in which two substantives are joined by a conjunction to express a single, complex idea. There is an unusually large number in *Hamlet*, for example: 'law and heraldry' (I.1.87), 'perfume and suppliance' (I.3.8), 'youth and observation', (I.5.101), 'encompassment and drift' (II.1.10) and 'amazement and admiration' (III.2.296)

lyrical song-like, melodious, such as Horatio's beautiful description of sunrise:

> But look, the morn, in russet mantle clad
> Walks o'er the dew of yon high eastern hill.   (I.1.166–7)

parody the imitation of a work of art usually intended to make fun of it by exaggerating its weaknesses. Thus Bardolph in *Henry V* deliberately mocks King Henry's patriotic speech, 'Once more unto the breech, dear friends, once more' with 'On, on, on, on, on! To the breach, to the breach!' (Act III Scenes 1 and 2)

pastiche a composition made up of bits and pieces of an original work, or a piece written in a manner pointedly resembling another's style. The Pyrrhus speech (Act 11 scene 2 ll 425ff) recited by the First Player deliberately recalls the overblown rhetorical manner of Shakespeare's younger contemporary, Christopher Marlowe

pathos a sense of grief, pity, loss. Ophelia's 'pretty madness' (IV.5) and Gertrude's subsequent account of her drowning (IV.7) are clearly intended to evoke feelings of pathos in the audience

psychoanalysis the study of the ways in which the workings of the 'unconscious' or subconscious mind influence our behaviour. It was pioneered in Vienna by Sigmund Freud whose first major work, *The Interpretation of Dreams* was published in 1900. Freud's challenge to accepted notions of character, motivation and belief was as revolutionary as Einstein's and Darwin's in their respective fields and contributed to the climate of radical scepticism characteristic of twentieth and twenty-first century thought. Many of Freud's theories derived from his studies of literature and mythology. Most notoriously, he saw the

Oedipus myth as illuminating every child's relationship with its parents. One of Freud's disciples, Ernst Jones published a study of *Hamlet*, called *Hamlet and Oedipus* which enjoyed a considerable vogue for a while and largely shaped the way Olivier presented the play in his film

Quarto a paper and book size; a printer's sheet is folded twice to make four leaves (eight pages). Several of Shakespeare's plays were printed in quarto size. The 1604 Quarto of *Hamlet* is now considered to be Shakespeare's first version of the play

revenge hero the protagonist of a **revenge tragedy**

revenge tragedy a special form of tragedy which concentrates on the protagonist's pursuit of private vengeance against those who have done him wrong. These plays often concentrate on the moral confusion caused by the need to answer evil with evil

set piece an episode, such as Gertrude's account of Ophelia's drowning (IV.7.166ff) or Hamlet's exchange with Osric (V.2.88–161) , which could almost stand alone as dramatically satisfying in its own right

soliloquy a dramatic convention which allows a character in a play to speak directly to the audience about his motives, feelings and decisions as if he were thinking aloud. Part of the convention is that a soliloquy provides accurate access to the character's innermost thoughts: we learn more about the character than could ever be gathered from the action of the play alone

tableau a dramatic, often symbolic arrangement of characters on stage. Thus our first sight of Claudius's brightly-lit court with Hamlet alone in mourning (1.2), *Hamlet*'s addressing Yorrick's skull (V.1.156–69) and the 'quarry' of dead bodies which Fortibras encounters when he enters at the end of the play (V.2.340ff.) add considerable weight to the words which are spoken

AUTHORS OF THESE NOTES

Jeff and Lynn Wood have written numerous textbooks. They are best known for *The Cambridge Poetry Workshop* and *The Cambridge Critical Workshop*, published by Cambridge University Press. Both have taught in a wide variety of secondary schools and in Cambridge sixth form colleges.

General editors

Martin Gray, former Head of the Department of English Studies at the University of Stirling, and of Literary Studies at the University of Luton

Professor A. N. Jeffares, Emeritus Professor of English, University of Stirling

Maya Angelou
I Know Why the Caged Bird Sings

Jane Austen
Pride and Prejudice

Alan Ayckbourn
Absent Friends

Elizabeth Barrett Browning
Selected Poems

Robert Bolt
A Man for All Seasons

Harold Brighouse
Hobson's Choice

Charlotte Brontë
Jane Eyre

Emily Brontë
Wuthering Heights

Shelagh Delaney
A Taste of Honey

Charles Dickens
David Copperfield
Great Expectations
Hard Times
Oliver Twist

Roddy Doyle
Paddy Clarke Ha Ha Ha

George Eliot
Silas Marner
The Mill on the Floss

Anne Frank
The Diary of a Young Girl

William Golding
Lord of the Flies

Oliver Goldsmith
She Stoops to Conquer

Willis Hall
The Long and the Short and the Tall

Thomas Hardy
Far from the Madding Crowd
The Mayor of Casterbridge
Tess of the d'Urbervilles
The Withered Arm and other Wessex Tales

L.P. Hartley
The Go-Between

Seamus Heaney
Selected Poems

Susan Hill
I'm the King of the Castle

Barry Hines
A Kestrel for a Knave

Louise Lawrence
Children of the Dust

Harper Lee
To Kill a Mockingbird

Laurie Lee
Cider with Rosie

Arthur Miller
The Crucible
A View from the Bridge

Robert O'Brien
Z for Zachariah

Frank O'Connor
My Oedipus Complex and Other Stories

George Orwell
Animal Farm

J.B. Priestley
An Inspector Calls
When We Are Married

Willy Russell
Educating Rita
Our Day Out

J.D. Salinger
The Catcher in the Rye

William Shakespeare
Henry IV Part I
Henry V
Julius Caesar
Macbeth
The Merchant of Venice
A Midsummer Night's Dream
Much Ado About Nothing

Romeo and Juliet
The Tempest
Twelfth Night

George Bernard Shaw
Pygmalion

Mary Shelley
Frankenstein

R.C. Sherriff
Journey's End

Rukshana Smith
Salt on the snow

John Steinbeck
Of Mice and Men

Robert Louis Stevenson
Dr Jekyll and Mr Hyde

Jonathan Swift
Gulliver's Travels

Robert Swindells
Daz 4 Zoe

Mildred D. Taylor
Roll of Thunder, Hear My Cry

Mark Twain
Huckleberry Finn

James Watson
Talking in Whispers

Edith Wharton
Ethan Frome

William Wordsworth
Selected Poems

A Choice of Poets

Mystery Stories of the Nineteenth Century including The Signalman

Nineteenth Century Short Stories

Poetry of the First World War

Six Women Poets

For the AQA Anthology:
Duffy and Armitage & Pre-1914 Poetry

Heaney and Clarke & Pre-1914 Poetry

Poems from Different Cultures

Margaret Atwood
Cat's Eye
The Handmaid's Tale

Jane Austen
Emma
Mansfield Park
Persuasion
Pride and Prejudice
Sense and Sensibility

Alan Bennett
Talking Heads

William Blake
*Songs of Innocence and of
Experience*

Charlotte Brontë
Jane Eyre
Villette

Emily Brontë
Wuthering Heights

Angela Carter
Nights at the Circus

Geoffrey Chaucer
The Franklin's Prologue and Tale
*The Merchant's Prologue and
Tale*
The Miller's Prologue and Tale
*The Prologue to the Canterbury
Tales*
*The Wife of Bath's Prologue and
Tale*

Samuel Coleridge
Selected Poems

Joseph Conrad
Heart of Darkness

Daniel Defoe
Moll Flanders

Charles Dickens
Bleak House
Great Expectations
Hard Times

Emily Dickinson
Selected Poems

John Donne
Selected Poems

Carol Ann Duffy
Selected Poems

George Eliot
Middlemarch
The Mill on the Floss

T.S. Eliot
Selected Poems
The Waste Land

F. Scott Fitzgerald
The Great Gatsby

E.M. Forster
A Passage to India

Brian Friel
Translations

Thomas Hardy
Jude the Obscure
The Mayor of Casterbridge
The Return of the Native
Selected Poems
Tess of the d'Urbervilles

Seamus Heaney
*Selected Poems from 'Opened
Ground'*

Nathaniel Hawthorne
The Scarlet Letter

Homer
The Iliad
The Odyssey

Aldous Huxley
Brave New World

Kazuo Ishiguro
The Remains of the Day

Ben Jonson
The Alchemist

James Joyce
Dubliners

John Keats
Selected Poems

Philip Larkin
*The Whitsun Weddings and
Selected Poems*

Christopher Marlowe
Doctor Faustus
Edward II

Arthur Miller
Death of a Salesman

John Milton
Paradise Lost Books I & II

Toni Morrison
Beloved

George Orwell
Nineteen Eighty-Four

Sylvia Plath
Selected Poems

Alexander Pope
*Rape of the Lock & Selected
Poems*

William Shakespeare
Antony and Cleopatra
As You Like It
Hamlet
Henry IV Part I
King Lear
Macbeth
Measure for Measure
The Merchant of Venice
A Midsummer Night's Dream
Much Ado About Nothing
Othello
Richard II
Richard III
Romeo and Juliet
The Taming of the Shrew
The Tempest
Twelfth Night
The Winter's Tale

George Bernard Shaw
Saint Joan

Mary Shelley
Frankenstein

Jonathan Swift
*Gulliver's Travels and A Modest
Proposal*

Alfred Tennyson
Selected Poems

Virgil
The Aeneid

Alice Walker
The Color Purple

Oscar Wilde
*The Importance of Being
Earnest*

Tennessee Williams
A Streetcar Named Desire
The Glass Menagerie

Jeanette Winterson
*Oranges Are Not the Only
Fruit*

John Webster
The Duchess of Malfi

Virginia Woolf
To the Lighthouse

William Wordsworth
*The Prelude and Selected
Poems*

W.B. Yeats
Selected Poems

Metaphysical Poets